REDLiGHT

When God Says No

Dr Shelly Cameron

To those patiently waiting on God's will

This book is dedicated to RJ, whose request inspired its creation and to Xavier, whose prayers breathed life into its words.

To Monique and Ashleigh May your hearts always be open to following the Lord's divine plan.

If you find yourself today where God is seemingly silent, don't think that He is not active.

What God is doing is rearranging the stage behind the scenes in your life and at just the

right time, the curtain will rise and you will be perfectly positioned to accomplish His

will, His purpose, His mission, and His vision for your life.

~ The Rev. Eric Yeakel

Contents

Preface 1

Introduction 3

How to Read This Book 6

When God Says No 7

Wisdom Unearthed: Insights from Biblical Icons .. 22

The Unraveling: Navigating Life's Turmoils 41

Encounters with Servant Leaders: Stories of
Inspiration 53

Igniting Hope: A Call to Courage and Resilience .. 67

Fear: Confusion Is Nothing New 81

Have Faith, Hope and Trust 95

Do All Things Through Christ 108

Conquer as the Spirit Leads 119

Solitude 135

The Power of Prayer 146

Give Thanks 164

Reset 171

Resources 182

Prayer For Salvation 183

15 Verses to Fight Fear 184

Other Books by Dr Shelly Cameron 186

About the Author 187

10-Year-Old RJ's Written Napkin Note to Write
this book 189

Thanks for Reading! 190

Preface

This book is the final in the GreenLight series. It was born from my long commute to a consulting client, which took two hours round trip. As I rushed out at 6:00 each morning, I would ask the Lord to give me the green light. One day, I realized that green lights only come when you are on the road. That is how my journey began.

I authored an inspirational book titled *"GreenLight: When God Says Go"* as I reflected. Two years later, I penned another book titled *"My Safe Place,"* which delved into moments of refuge when God tells us to slow down. This can happen when we lose a loved one, face unforeseen challenges, suffer job loss, witness relationships deteriorate, or simply when life spirals out of control. In such situations, God may tell us to slow down or pause because He remains in control.

"RedLight" is the last book in the series. It came through the innocence of a child's handwritten scribble on a napkin. My daughter's 10-year-old son, RJ, handed me the napkin, giggling, and requested that I write it. The message intrigued me, and I looked up to the Lord with a smile. I couldn't ignore it, as it seemed like a divine message. I willingly surrendered to the Lord's leadership. Incidentally, the prequel, My *Safe Place,* was being published. Who am I to disobey as the 'traffic light' trilogy unfolds?

That's how God speaks—but we must be listening. God speaks to us in whispers, through playful notes, and during moments of serene surrender. He invites us to listen and heed the signals directing our path.

Introduction

In an instant, a young mother's world was shattered as she experienced a chilling nightmare. Her husband acted violently in an attempted murder-suicide, which left her with seven shots piercing her body. He suffered a self-inflicted single bullet that pierced his head. Miraculously, she survived, but the haunting memories of that fateful night remain etched into her very soul. As the dust settled, her husband succumbed to his fatal shot, leaving her to endure the harrowing aftermath as it had unfolded before her young children. This was a story that shocked the public at daybreak one bleak morning, gripping their hearts and souls. It left loved ones grappling with grief and sorrow as they searched for a glimmer of hope in the darkness.

This true story was a heart-pounding moment that froze time as tragedy struck, reminding us of life's delicate unpredictability. Amidst the haunting echoes of devastation, we cry out to God, and question His divine plan. How do we find meaning when confronted with such overwhelming despair? How do we cope with the grief that envelops us? We implore and plead, wondering why inevitable tragedies unfold, why innocence is taken, and why senseless suffering occurs.

Upon reflection, we recognize that life is full of diverse signs. Sometimes, the Lord encourages us to move forward confidently, while at other times, He cautions us to slow down or proceed with caution. Then, there are moments when He sends a clear message to stop—to pause, reassess, and wait. Yet, we often ignore the cautionary signs, eager to rush ahead like a car at an intersection, longing for the green light to go. We forget that sometimes God's red light commands us to stop for our own safety, protection, and well-being. Faced with these impenetrable mysteries, we grapple with the truth that sometimes God says no.

Today, the message is simple: It's time to pause, step out of the frantic race, and silence the rushing thoughts. In this book, we are called to discover the beauty of stopping—to reflect, learn, and find solace in the Lord's guidance.

So, dear reader, as you embark on this transformative journey, may it inspire you to embrace life's divine signals. Heed the red light, find solace in the yellow, and confidently move ahead with the green. The "traffic light" trilogy teaches us to listen, which is how God speaks and reveals life's most profound meaning. The trilogy is more than a series of books; it is a testament to how God speaks to us.

How to Read This Book

As with the other books in the GreenLight series, in the contents of this book, I share a few of my experiences and those of others I have encountered. Readers can expect to glide through comfort, encouragement, confusion, guidance on decision-making, where to find peace, and more.

Read a few at a time, or a day at a time. The goal is to help you stay close to the Lord even when He says no or to wait. A psalm or a proverb is featured between chapters. The Book of Psalms emphasizes the importance of praising our Heavenly Father. The Proverbs teach wisdom for daily living.

Therefore, seek the Lord when life becomes challenging and you become afraid. He is your safe place. Please slow down during stressful and overwhelming times and seek comfort in Him. Then listen for the green light when He tells you to get up and go.

I hope this book not only inspires you to seek solace in Him during the tough seasons but also encourages you to draw near to Him during those times of joy. May it guide those who patiently await God's will with hope, faith, and trust.

Blessings overflow.

When God Says No

If the request is wrong, God says 'No.'
If the timing is wrong, God says 'Slow.'
If you are wrong, God says 'Grow.'
But if the request is right and the timing is right
and you are right,
God says 'Go.'

~ Bill Hybel

Wow! I Ran the Red Light

In the heart-pounding world of rush hour, where every second counts, I found myself facing an impossible choice. The morning sun had barely risen above the horizon. As I approached the intersection, my pulse quickened. The traffic light ahead beckoned like a beacon of hope in vibrant green.

But this was peak hour, a time when the city became congested, leading to a bottleneck of frustration and impatience. A car up ahead navigated the road with all the urgency of a snail, testing the limits of my patience.

Then it happened.

Out of nowhere, a rogue driver appeared like a phantom of recklessness and audacity. With a swiftness that defied reason, the driver cut into my lane like an intruder on a mission to disrupt the balance of my meticulously planned morning. The realization hit me like a ton of bricks—I was going to be late for a crucial meeting that could make or break my day.

Disappointment settled in my chest, soon joined by simmering anger. The green light, once a symbol of promise, shifted ominously. It transformed into an impatient shade of yellow, an ominous countdown to impending doom.

Time seemed to stand still as I raced against the clock, clinging to the steering wheel. The light, now betraying me, was poised to plunge into an incriminating red. I could not let it happen. Not today, not with so much at stake. But destiny hung in the balance as I hurtled toward that ever-narrowing gap. Would I make it, defying the odds and the inexplicable audacity of others? Or would the crushing weight of unnecessary delays trap me?

With every ounce of determination, I floored the accelerator as a torrent of emotions propelled me forward. The world blurred into a stream of frustration and fury, but I wouldn't yield. I had a meeting to make, a job to keep, and an indomitable will to navigate the chaos of the morning commute.

Sigh. Encouraging my girls and friends to drive with caution is my priority. To be patient. Yet I ended up doing the same thing. So often, it is the same reaction that causes serious accidents. But I am thankful I got lucky. Even though I knew better, I did not act accordingly.

How often do you experience moments like this while pursuing your daily goals or spending time with God? For me, it was the distance and the urgency to get to my meeting on time. For you, it may be goals such as further studies, marriage, starting a family, a career change, purchasing a house or car for the first time, or something else. Then things go awry, and we hesitate. Sometimes, we give up, thinking we've erred so much that the Lord no longer cares.

Today, I encourage you to never give up. Hold on to the Lord Almighty. Through Him, be strong and keep going. You will be glad you did.

"Cast your burden on the LORD, and he will sustain you; he will never permit the righteous to be moved" (Psalm 55:22).

When Everything Stops

When everything comes to a halt, or rather, when everything ought to stop. More than a decade ago, I lost my grandmother, the matriarch of our family. The cancer had returned after three score and ten years. It did not stop her from being who she was—the be-all and end-all of our lives. But then, one day, the bank manager where I worked called me into her office, sat me down, and informed me that the hospital had called. My grandmother had passed away.

Perturbed, I looked around. Customers were still in the bank, walking around, conducting their daily business. I could not understand. For me, everything had stopped.

I reflect on what's happening around the world. Threats, wars, and natural disasters are rampant. Yet elsewhere, people continue their business as usual, posting on different social media platforms. It begs the question: Is there a bridge? Do we care? Yes, many people genuinely care. Benevolence saturates the heart, and for sure, with heightened economic downturns, the world will always feel the effects.

So, let's not give up hope because fear stops life, and love fades when we stop caring. You can rest assured that the Lord is in control, and nothing surprises Him.

"He will wipe every tear from their eyes.
There will be no more death or mourning or crying or pain,
for the old order of things has passed away" (Revelation 21:4
NIV).

Prayer Doesn't Work

Seven-year-old Xavier said, "Prayer doesn't work," after asking his parents for a dog before his seventh birthday. He did not believe he would get it, so I encouraged him to pray. He did. Eight months later, he apparently gave up after receiving many other gifts that he loved but no dog.

While driving home one day after church, he almost floored me when he said, "GranShell, prayer doesn't work." His softly spoken words surprised me and got me thinking. How many times as adults do we become disappointed in the Lord's unresponsiveness to our heartfelt pleas for something we consider necessary to us? What my grandson needed to know was that his parents were contemplating his request. However, owning a dog comes with many responsibilities. A few include considering the right breed (one that is hypoallergenic), covering dog care costs, including health insurance, and assessing his readiness for such a commitment.

A year later, his aunt got him a dog, which delighted him as he played with it. But he soon realized he hated walking the little beagle and later admitted that he was happy that he did not get a dog of his own.

The Lord does the same thing to us. He is answering our prayers, but He does so intending to provide the right things at the right time when we are truly prepared to receive them. We can think of biblical examples, such as Moses, who was tasked with leading the children of Israel to accomplish God's promises for them. However, the Lord's timing differed from Moses' expectations. The Lord took him away from Pharaoh's palace without notice to prepare Moses, and He sent him to become a simple shepherd. Years later, when Moses was genuinely prepared, the Lord used him to lead the children of Israel out of oppression.

Joseph is another compelling example. They innocently sent him to prison for a crime he had not committed. Joseph's trials were divinely ordered to prepare him for greater responsibilities. Ultimately, he assumed a crucial role in his country's food distribution during a severe famine.

Today, have confidence and know that the Lord is working on your behalf in His own way in due time. He has everything lined up to be presented at the perfect moment. Therefore, be patient and wait in faith.

"Many are the plans in a person's heart,
but it is the LORD's purpose that prevails" (Proverbs 19:21
NIV).

Oh, How I Long for Red Lights

As I wrote this book, I worked at an opportunity where my commute took me straight to the highway for about 60 miles each way. During this time, I began to reflect on how much I longed for red lights. This hit home.

In my previous book, "GreenLight: When God Says Go," I used to pray fervently for non-stop green traffic lights as I drove all the way east. Whenever those lights turned red, I would become frustrated because I wanted to keep moving forward. However, my perspective has since shifted. I now long for those moments when I can pause, switch to another audiobook, or simply take a break from the current one. I long for the opportunity to stop, acknowledge and observe my surroundings, and enjoy a cup of tea safely as I continue my drive. I longed to stop for a breather.

Personally, I don't understand how the Lord deals with us. We are never satisfied. He gives us the green light, and we complain because we want to stop. He gives us red lights, and we yearn to keep moving without interruption. He advises us to slow down and seek refuge in His safe place, and we say we have no time to stop. Oh, how persistently He patiently waits for us!

Lord, we thank you for Your endurance and patience with us.

"Look, as the clay is in the potter's hand, so are you in My hand, O house of Israel!" (Jeremiah 18:6 NKJV).

The Right Time

How often have you asked the Lord for something and He said no? No doubt, there are many times. In my childhood, I aspired to become a nurse because I enjoyed caring for others. But nursing was not my destined path. My career took a turn towards banking, where I developed a keen interest in People Management because of my role and responsibilities. Later, I switched to the pharmaceutical industry, managing people in leadership roles in different countries. Subsequently, I ventured into the healthcare sector, where I managed several clinics in different counties in South Florida.

Upon reflection, I believe the Lord's purpose was to place me in an area where I could more effectively impact patient care. It started in the pharmaceutical industry and then moved on to overseeing healthcare operations as an administrator.

In contrast, cancer claimed the lives of my mom, grandmother, and sister from our family despite our prayers for healing. Though I miss them terribly, His response was to provide them with spiritual healing, liberating them from the suffering of their earthly bodies. It was selfish of me to desire their continued presence while they endured such pain. The Lord knew the right time to call them home.

So, remember, sometimes God says yes. Other times, He says no. The one important thing we can do is trust Him. His plan is always the best for us. Take some time to reflect on the path He has taken you through. Decipher how, when, and where He gave you the green light. Did you miss any? If so, there is still time. Pray. Call upon Him. Trust His leadership.

"He went away a second time and prayed, "My Father, if it is not possible for this cup to be taken away unless I drink it, may your will be done" (Matthew 26:42 NIV).

God answers our prayers when we stop.

~ Sarah Jakes Roberts

PSALM 121

I lift up my eyes to the mountains—
  where does my help come from?
My help comes from the Lord,
  the Maker of heaven and earth.

He will not let your foot slip—
  he who watches over you will not slumber;
indeed, he who watches over Israel
  will neither slumber nor sleep.

The Lord watches over you—
  the Lord is your shade at your right hand;
the sun will not harm you by day,
  nor the moon by night.

The Lord will keep you from all harm—
  he will watch over your life;
the Lord will watch over your coming and going
  both now and forevermore.

Wisdom Unearthed: Insights from Biblical Icons

Joseph the Dreamer Rescued Jacob the Deceiver

I never cared too much for Jacob because he stole his brother Esau's birthright. As I matured, I realized he was Joseph's father, the son I adored. Jacob went through many trials throughout his life. Jacob loved Rachel and worked for seven years to marry her, but her father tricked him into marrying her older sister. Love conquered all when he worked another seven years for the woman he loved. Rachel was Joseph's mother, and Jacob loved Joseph more than anyone else. The challenge? This affection was widely known among his brothers.

From an early age, Joseph was a dreamer. God gave Joseph a dream that he would achieve great things and that his brothers would bow down to him. Silly Joseph did not keep his mouth shut and shared his dream with his older brothers. Sadly, they did not understand the ways of the Lord. Jealousy led his brothers to plot to kill Joseph's dream. Their theory coerced them into believing that if they killed him, then his dream would die with him.

But God's ways are not our ways. Instead of killing him, Joseph's brothers sold him, unknowingly playing a part in the Lord's direct plan and purpose for Joseph's life. As Jacob mourned, Potiphar, the captain of Pharaoh's guard, bought Joseph. Potiphar favored Joseph and put him in charge of his house. Joseph held responsibility for everything. A handsome man, Joseph caught the affection of Potiphar's wife, who one day made advances towards him. Joseph rejected her advances and made a hasty retreat, leaving his cloak behind. She used this as twisted evidence against him. Sadly, authorities imprisoned Joseph for many years because of false accusations from Potiphar's wife.

However, Joseph found favor wherever he went— even in jail. The dreamer, Joseph, interpreted the dreams of two inmates and asked one to remember him when he was released. The former inmate did, but not until years later, when the Pharaoh needed a dream interpreted. With the Lord's help, Joseph interpreted the dream and was responsible for being the second in charge of the land of Egypt. Oh, what a miracle!

Joseph's brothers eventually bowed down to him not only once but several times. Joseph also reunited with his father, Jacob, the deceiver, who had himself been deceived many times.

Was this a wasted life? Absolutely not. Joseph's life was one of integrity, resilience, respect, and honor. He rescued his dad in his sunset years and overcame many challenges to accomplish the Lord's supreme plan and purpose.

What are you waiting for? Take note: The Lord may be long, but He is always on time. Wait for the Lord's plan and purpose for your life. Hold on to Him. Pray. Gain the strength He provides to see you through. Always have faith that a rejection from God could lead to a better outcome.

"Wait for the Lord; be strong and take heart and wait for the Lord" (Psalm 27:14 NIV).

Pray Like David

Run like Joseph! That was the outburst from my young adult daughter during a conversation with a youth group. They were discussing the temptations that exist in our society. She based her response on how David handled Bathsheba's seduction.

When life becomes challenging, I recommend praying as David did. David consistently sought the Lord's guidance before making any decision, never taking a step without consulting Him. He did something by first asking the Lord's direction. He prayed to the Lord for guidance on whether he should pursue his enemy, make certain moves, engage in battles, or flee.

David then listened for the Lord's leading, and as He obeyed, he consistently enjoyed the fruits of success. Let's pray to God for help in any situation. It may be decision-making, entrepreneurship, relationships, finances, or mental struggles. Then, wait as you listen for His answer. As you obey His guidance and direction, be sure that you will enjoy success.

The Lord is always on time, so be encouraged and keep praying as David did.

"I will stand at my watch and station myself on the ramparts; I will look to see what he will say to me, and what answer I am to give to this complaint" (Habakkuk 2:1 NIV).

God Says Go. Jonah Said No

Has the Lord ever told you to do something you did not want to do? Perhaps it was leaving a toxic relationship or quitting a stressful job with no alternative income in sight. It could even involve relocating to a new place where you have no friends or family—a risky endeavor indeed.

Jonah experienced one such divine instruction. God commanded Jonah to go to the great city of Nineveh and preach against it because of its wickedness. Jonah, however, disagreed with sparing their lives, so he ran in the opposite direction. He boarded a ship, hoping to escape God's will. Yet, a fierce storm arose, tossing the ship back and forth and scaring everyone on board. Eventually, Jonah confessed to the ship's crew and asked to be thrown into the sea. He landed in the belly of a fish. For days and nights, Jonah prayed. The prodigal prophet was spit upon dry land, as faith would have it. Oh, what miracles God bestows!

As Calvary's Pastor Mike Wiggins puts it, "God said go, and Jonah said no."

When we say no to the Lord's instructions, let us be prepared for the consequences. God's purpose will be accomplished with or without our help.

Heading downward is the path we choose when we run away from the Lord. Remember, He is everywhere. Nothing on earth can hide us from the face of God, who sees all and knows all.

Surrender to Him today.

"Where can I go from your Spirit? Where can I flee from your presence?
If I go up to the heavens, you are there; if I make my bed in the depths, you are there.
If I rise on the wings of the dawn, if I settle on the far side of the sea,
even there your hand will guide me, your right hand will hold me fast" (Psalm 139:7-10 NIV).

Abraham Not Isaac

One day, God told Abraham to take his one and only son, Isaac, and offer him up as a sacrifice. Wow! Wouldn't that be the most challenging task ever? Yet Abraham obeyed. Believe it or not, he got up early in the morning to do just that. Many of us would have delayed cherishing every minute with our only son. I know I would have, but not Abraham. In obedience, he got up early, loaded his donkey, and took two of his servants with him to the place God had instructed.

Young Isaac, in confusion, asked his father Abraham where the lamb for the burned offering was. He could clearly see the fire and wood, but no lamb. Abraham, (praying) confidently replied that God will provide.

"Then he reached out his hand and took the knife to slay his son. But the angel of the Lord called out to him from heaven, "Abraham! Abraham!" "Here I am," he replied. "Do not lay a hand on the boy," he said. "Do not do anything to him. Now I know you fear God, because you have not withheld from me your son, your only son" (Genesis 22:10–12 NIV).

Was Isaac afraid? Moreso, was Abraham? Yes, I believe both were afraid. After all, Abraham was like you and me. The difference was that he did not let fear stop him. He stepped forward in faith, believing that God's promises would come to pass. Boy, that was some faith.

Abraham must have felt immense relief when he heard the voice of the Lord. There, a lamb miraculously appeared, caught in the thicket. The instructions were to slay the lamb instead. Oh, the joy Abraham must have felt! God had come through.

The lesson for us is to follow the Lord's leading. He will provide in His time. At the right time, He came through when Isaac was bound and was just about to be slain as the burnt offering.

Today, let's obey and watch the Lord work things out according to His will and purpose for our lives.

"Bring the whole tithe into the storehouse, that there may be food in my house. Test me in this," says the Lord Almighty, "and see if I will not throw open the floodgates of heaven and pour out so much blessing that there will not be room enough to store it" (Malachi 3:10 NIV).

Hope Shattered a 3-Day Nightmare...

When Saul was struck blind, I can only imagine what he went through. Just imagine a healthy person with a great job going about his business, a hard worker, diligent in all he did, and dedicated to persecuting Christians who spoke about the Lord. In a moment, everything turned dark for him, and he was blinded.

I can only imagine the hell he went through. Call 911! Would he ever be able to see things again? Panic set in; he couldn't see anything. He was so far away from home, traveling. Who could he rely on to come and assist him? Would it take days for help to arrive? How could he live with this shame? This sudden disability? Without warning, he was blinded.

But God had a plan.

While Saul was worried, he also prayed. A strange new thing for him. He had no choice but to call out to the voice he heard while on the road to Damascus.

God sent a man, Ananias, despite his fear of Saul, the persecutor of Christians. It was a risk, but he obeyed and went. God the Almighty took care of the fears of both Saul and Ananias. Days later, Saul believed and was healed. In a moment, his sight returned. Suddenly, after days of hell, his mission changed. With a renewed sense of purpose, he promised to suffer for Christ's sake.

Today, if you are afraid of what's happening in your life, take comfort in knowing that God always has a plan for what you and I are going through. It's hard, but when you are going through difficulties, whether or not you caused them, talk to the Lord. He will see you through. Always trust Him.

Saul, the persecutor, became Paul, the pursuer. Indeed, God has a sense of humor. Trust Him.

"But the Lord said, "Go, for Saul is my chosen instrument to take my message to the Gentiles and to kings, as well as to the people of Israel. And I will show him how much he must suffer for my name's sake" (Acts 9:15-16 NLT).

Bathsheba Look Up

Could Bathsheba have said no? When David approached Bathsheba through his servant, could she have refused? Chances are, she did not know why he summoned her. Bathsheba was Uriah the Hittite's wife and she later married David.

The story is told of David, who witnessed Bathsheba as she lazed in her courtyard, taking a bath. Clean herself, the Bible says. A woman of noble character, Bathsheba innocently cleaned herself in the privacy of her home with no fear of anyone seeing her. But she forgot to look up; had she done so, she might have spotted David at the far-off heights of his own court.

Her beauty incited lust—a desire that causes many to fail. Males and females alike fall victim to its prey. How can we forget about Pharaoh's wife, who pursued and falsely accused Joseph out of lust when he rejected her?

But, like Joseph, could Bathsheba have run away? The Bible is silent on this matter. The Lord held both David and Bathsheba accountable for their actions. They both lost their beloved son, struck with sickness that led to his death.

In less than a year, Bathsheba went through various emotions as she tried to recover. She was most likely perplexed by her relationship with King David, followed by the loss of her husband, Uriah, and later her newborn baby. What a roller coaster year that was!

As parents, both David and Bathsheba prayed for God to heal their child, but God said no. They had to suffer the consequences of their actions. Later, God intervened and blessed David and Bathsheba with another child, who became known as Solomon, the wisest man ever to live.

Sometimes, God says no, even when we plead for help, but His purpose is wiser than our folly and immediate desires. He knows the future. Did you do something wrong? No matter what, seek forgiveness and, in humility, bear the consequences. Seek forgiveness and have faith that God will come through for you.

"The wicked draw the sword and bend the bow to bring down the poor and needy, to slay those whose ways are upright" (Psalm 37:14 NIV).

Moses

Moses' mother was a woman of divine wisdom. Pharoah ordered that they throw all baby boys into the river Nile, but Moses' mother pondered how she could obey while preserving her baby's life. She found the answer in a watertight basket left in the river while his sister watched from a distance.

Miraculously, Pharoah's daughter found the basket, leading to a conversation with the baby's sister. Moses' own mom was asked to nurse the child. They took him to Pharaoh's house after he was weaned, and he grew up being exposed to the best education, life, and more.

One day after a murderous act, Moses escaped to tend a flock, despite his previous influential position in Pharoah's house. Moses was humbled, but God never forgot him. He received strength and divine favor from God to lead the children of Israel en route to the promised land. The wonder of wonders from the river He came, and through the river He led the children of Israel out of Egypt.

Consider Moses when you think about what is happening in your life. Whether it is confusion, apathy, fear, or sadness. Take inspiration from Moses as you contemplate what's happening in your life. Leave all your troubles to God. He works everything out for your good, both the important things and the small ones.

May you continue to trust Him.

"When the child grew older, she took him to Pharaoh's daughter and he became her son. She named him Moses, saying, "I drew him out of the water" (Exodus 2:10 NIV).

Nick Vujicic

Born without legs

"The nurses were crying. The midwife was crying. And of course, I was crying! Finally, they put me next to her, still covered, and my mum just couldn't bear what she was seeing: her child without limbs. Take him away, she said. I don't want to touch him or see him" (Nick Vujicic, Life Without Limits).

That was the first reaction from Nick Vujicic's mother. He was born without limbs. No hands. No feet. Phocomelia, as it is called, and his mother, a nurse who delivered hundreds of babies, was in shock. There were no warning signs during the pregnancy, and now that the baby was here, she was stunned. His father's reaction was almost to topple over. He had to be escorted from the delivery room. When he recovered, he exclaimed to the pediatrician, "My son has no arms," to which the doctor responded sensitively, 'Your son has neither arms nor legs'. His father went weak with shock and anguish.

Indeed, a shock to any parent, this man, whom God chose not to give legs or arms, has significantly impacted the world. He has inspired many. He swims. Plays golf. He became a renowned worldwide speaker.

"Do you know why I love God?" Nick Vujicic asked a young girl on stage who was born without arms and legs like him "Because Heaven is real. And one day, when we get to Heaven, we are going to have arms and legs. And we are going to run, and we are going to play, and we are going to race."

There is always hope when we trust God.

"The LORD is my rock, my fortress and my deliverer., my God, my rock, in whom I take refuge, my shield, and the horn of my salvation, my stronghold" (Psalm 18:2 NIV).

PROVERBS 3

A good name is more desirable than great riches;
 to be esteemed is better than silver or gold.

Rich and poor have this in common:
 The Lord is the Maker of them all.

The prudent see danger and take refuge,
 but the simple keep going and pay the penalty.

Humility is the fear of the Lord;
 its wages are riches and honor and life.

In the paths of the wicked are snares and pitfalls,
 but those who would preserve their life stay far
 from them.

Start children off on the way they should go,
 and even when they are old they will not turn
 from it.

The rich rule over the poor,
 and the borrower is slave to the lender.

Whoever sows injustice reaps calamity,
 and the rod they wield in fury will be broken.

The generous will themselves be blessed,
   for they share their food with the poor.

Drive out the mocker, and out goes strife;
   quarrels and insults are ended.

One who loves a pure heart and who speaks with grace
   will have the king for a friend.

The eyes of the Lord keep watch over knowledge,
   but he frustrates the words of the unfaithful.

The sluggard says, "There's a lion outside!
   I'll be killed in the public square!"

The mouth of an adulterous woman is a deep pit;
   a man who is under the Lord's wrath falls into it.

Folly is bound up in the heart of a child,
   but the rod of discipline will drive it far away.

One who oppresses the poor to increase his wealth
   and one who gives gifts to the rich—both come to poverty

The Unraveling:
Navigating Life's Turmoils

Slow Down

When you can't see clearly, slow down or even stop. The news reported sisters returning from a trip to Disneyland. The driver, a young mom in her early 20s, could hardly see because of the immense fog and rain. She sped up to get past the fog, but sadly, she drove head-on into another car, which caused two fatalities. One family member said they couldn't see clearly, which caused the accident.

It's important to be cautious and avoid worrying or panicking. If you are building a business, studying for a college degree, building a family, planning a vacation getaway, or pursuing any goal, take your time. You may need to slow down or even stop when you cannot see your way clearly. It is only wise. Accelerating and going full speed ahead can be dangerous. At times, you may need to pause and reflect. Are you on track? Is it still even applicable? If you are not paying attention and things change, it is necessary to recoup and see if you need to change direction, make a U-turn, or try something new.

Today, I encourage you to open your eyes wide. Obey the Lord's leading and strive to discern the path He guides you along. Are you still on track?

"God is our refuge and strength, an ever-present help in trouble" (Psalm 46:1 NIV).

Closed Doors

A famous saying is that "whenever God shuts one door, He opens a window." The most typical reason for using this remark is to reassure someone after they have missed an opportunity. When facing job loss, the end of a relationship, or the departure of loved ones, people often use the phrase, "When God closes a door, He opens a window."

When I moved to a new area years ago, the pastor mentioned that a highly involved family had just moved to another region. I smiled softly because our previous church had also mourned our leaving for this new place. Our family used to volunteer actively at the church. Our stay with that church had lasted over ten years. We took part in everything, including holding several leadership roles simultaneously. God had opened a window for that church by using our willingness to serve.

The late Dr. Charles Stanley provided a commentary on Closed Doors.

- *Closed doors prevent mistakes.* Just because a path is clear doesn't mean it's the one God intends for us to follow. Sometimes, we will need more information to make a wise decision, so He blocks the way. The Holy Spirit knows the complete road map for our lives, so we should follow Him.

- *Closed doors redirect our walk.* God won't leave a willing servant with nothing to do.

- *Closed doors can result* in better fruit, more satisfaction, and greater glory for Him.

- *Closed doors test faith and build perseverance.* Waiting for the Lord is hard, but it is a means by which we can learn wisdom, patience, and trust.

- *Closed doors buy us time.* We are only sometimes as prepared as we would like to think. God may temporarily shut down an opportunity for service until we are ready.

Closed doors offer many opportunities for us to learn. We often get disappointed with delays when we pray to the Lord for our needs and desires. Our impatience sometimes hinders our ability to learn. Then, later, we found we needed more time to be ready for the opportunity. So, despite the challenges faced, remember that God's ways are not ours, but He knows best. If we keep pushing forward and follow His guidance, He will help us overcome. Be encouraged to always trust Him because His promises are true and His mercies are new every morning.

Dear Lord, grant us the precious gift of patience to wait for your perfect timing.

"See, I have placed before you an open door that no one can shut. I know that you have little strength, yet you have kept my word and have not denied my name" (Revelation 3:8 NIV).

Quietly Quitting

"I'll just skip it". My daughter's 9-year-old told me He was talking about brushing his teeth that night. It was so sudden and unexpected that I laughed aloud. Quietly quitting, it's called.

It's a post-pandemic phenomenon that The Times Magazine referred to as the concept of no longer going above and beyond and instead doing what employees' job descriptions require of them and only that. 'Quiet Quitting' is seen by employees as establishing boundaries. Companies fear the long-term effects.

I reflect on its application to our walk with the Lord. Too often, we quietly quit. Often, we do not express it but simply act on it. When we are too busy to pray, read the Bible, or do devotions, it's because we're only doing the bare minimum. Then, as our time with the Lord dwindles, we find ourselves spiritually weak. Before long, the days turn into weeks, months, and even years. Our strength fades away, and our lives lose meaning. If we go to church, we do it more out of obligation than out of worship. We neglect our spiritual lives until we are compelled to stop.

May we receive the wisdom to follow the Lord's lead and stay in tune with Him.

"This Book of the Law shall not depart from your mouth, but you shall meditate on it day and night, so that you may be careful to do according to all that is written in it. For then you will make your way prosperous, and then you will have good success" (John 1:8 ESV).

Unraveling a Chaotic Day:
My Tale of Misadventures

Have you ever experienced one of those days where everything conspires against you? Let me take you through one experience as I recount one such unforgettable day. My boss and I got into a heated argument, which sparked a storm because of their own conflict with higher-ups in the hierarchy. Little did I know that this was just the opening act of a symphony of misfortunes.

As the sun set below the horizon, I embarked on a frantic mission to return an upgraded phone to the post office. Alas, my haste led to oversight, and the device's settings remained untouched. I sat in my car, steadfastly attempting to reset the obstinate device while feeling a mixture of frustration and resolve. Time slipped through my fingers like sand as 45 minutes elapsed, leaving me rushing into the post office just before their closing hour. However, life's irony had something else in store for me.

As I struggled with the device, it slowly dawned on me that the box I held was meant for UPS, not USPS. The clerk's quiet revelation stunned me. Yet an unexpected reaction bubbled up from within me—laughter. How could I not chuckle at the absurdity of it all?

Still reeling from these escapades, I found myself facing a technical nightmare just before a live event. My heart sank, mirroring my sinking confidence. Seeking refuge from the chaos, I ventured to the grocery store, determined to exchange an item. But that, too, went awry, for it met me with yet another roadblock. My efforts met resistance at every turn, and my day spiraled into a series of mishaps that left me questioning the forces at play.

Defeated, I returned home, clutching my phone, which had become a symbol of my thwarted endeavors. As the night turned into day, a tragedy was revealed that made my own problems pale in comparison. A family—parents, twin teenagers, and another innocent soul—met their untimely end in a catastrophic collision.

Their fate made me feel humbled and put my problems into perspective.

So, remember, no matter what, there is always someone going through something worse than you are. We will always experience good days and bad days. But we remain confident that the Lord remains with us in all our circumstances as He guards our hearts in perfect love. Take your burdens to the Lord and leave them there.

"Praise be to the Lord, to God our Savior, who daily bears our burdens" (Psalm 68:19 NIV).

All the Time in the World...

I overheard a discussion with professional medical personnel. The older adult couple commented that they were getting older. The young professional medical practitioner responded, "That's okay; we will be around for a while."

How can you be sure that you will be around for a while? Life is not promised. Let us be careful of our assumptions. The biblical story told of the rich man who planned to tear down and build bigger barns to store his crops, which he had reaped plentifully. He planned to be around for a long time. He planned to store goods for many years so he could relax, eat, drink, and be merry. Sadly, he passed away that very night.

So, think before you speak, because no one knows the future. People make plans, but God has the final say.

"This is what I'll do. I will tear down my barns and build bigger ones, and there I will store my surplus grain" (Luke 12:18 NIV).

PSALM 93

The Lord rules.
  He puts on majesty as if it were clothes.
  The Lord puts on majesty and strength.
Indeed, the world has been set in place.
  It is firm and secure.
Lord, you began to rule a long time ago.
  You have always existed.

Lord, the seas have lifted up their voice.
  They have lifted up their pounding waves.
But Lord, you are more powerful than the roar
of the ocean.
  You are stronger than the waves of the sea.
  Lord, you are powerful in heaven.

Your laws do not change, Lord.
  Your temple will be holy
  for all time to come.

Encounters with Servant Leaders: Stories of Inspiration

Peace Like a River

Horatio G. Spafford was a successful lawyer and businessman in Chicago with a lovely family—a wife, Anna, and five children. However, they were not strangers to tears and tragedy. Their young son died of pneumonia in 1871, and in that same year, much of their business was lost in the great Chicago fire. Yet God allowed the business to flourish again in His mercy and kindness.

On November 21, 1873, the French ocean liner Ville du Havre crossed the Atlantic from the U.S. to Europe with 313 passengers on board. Among the passengers were Mrs. Spafford and their four daughters. Although Mr. Spafford had planned to go with his family, he needed to stay in Chicago to help solve an unexpected business problem. He told his wife that he would join her and their children in Europe a few days later. He planned to take another ship.

About four days into the crossing of the Atlantic, the Ville du Harve collided with a mighty, iron-hulled Scottish ship, the Loch Earn. Suddenly, all of those on board were in grave danger. Anna hurriedly brought her four children to the deck. She knelt there with Annie, Margaret Lee, Bessie, and Tanetta and prayed that God would spare them if that could be His will or make them willing to endure whatever awaited them. Within approximately 12 minutes, the Ville du Harve slipped beneath the Atlantic's dark waters, carrying 226 passengers, including the four Spafford children.

A sailor, rowing a small boat over the spot where the ship went down, spotted a woman floating on a piece of the wreckage. It was Anna, still alive. He pulled her into the boat, and another large vessel picked them up, which, nine days later, landed them in Cardiff, Wales. From there, she wired her husband a message that began, "Saved alone, what shall I do?" Mr. Spafford later framed the telegram and placed it in his office.

Another of the ship's survivors, Pastor Weiss, later recalled Anna saying, "God gave me four daughters. Now they have been taken from me. Someday I will understand why."

Mr. Spafford booked passage on the next available ship and left to join his grieving wife. With the ship about four days out, the captain called Spafford to his cabin and told him they were over the place where his children went down.

According to Bertha Spafford Vester, a daughter born after the tragedy, Spafford wrote "It Is Well with My Soul" while on this journey.

When peace like a river attendeth my way,
When sorrows like sea billows roll,
Whatever my lot, thou hast taught me to say,
It is well, it is well with my soul.
It is well with my soul,
It is well, it is well with my soul.

May the story and hymn from St. Augustine's Record bring comfort and peace to those who mourn a loved one.

"And the peace of God which surpasses all understanding, will guard your hearts and minds through Christ Jesus" (Philippians 4:7 NKJV).

Some Die so Others Can Live. The Death That Created Success...

The difference some people make comes alive after they are gone. ~Dr. Shelly Cameron

Martin Luther King, Jr., was a Baptist minister and an extraordinary leader. His death catapulted a movement so others could live. Many national heroes and legendary leaders have made an impact through their deaths. Their deaths helped others live.

It causes us to wonder if some people are born with the purpose of making a difference after death. We think of children. They created Amber Alert when little Amber died after being abducted. It was sad, but her death encouraged changes that saved the lives of other children.

Sadly, it is in death that we understand. Only after some people die do we understand the purpose of life. Today, I encourage you to look back on your life. Try to understand your purpose. Are you on the path that is leading you to make a difference?

Reflect. Think about your purpose. Why are you here? While you are at it, remember to ponder Dr. Martin Luther King Jr.'s final "I Have a

Dream" speech. It depicted a leader who had attained his true purpose.

Think deeply about the Lord Jesus Christ and His life. Everything He did was to provide salvation for us at no cost. He gave us His own so that we could live. Accept His gift and follow Him today.

"So we make it our goal to please him, whether we are at home in the body or away from it" (2 Corinthians 5:9 NIV).

God's Plan

Every day, we're amazed by how God's plan prevails despite the wickedness in our society. Consider Moses, whom Pharoah meant to kill, yet he grew up right under his nose.

Joseph of Arimathea, a wealthy man, comes to mind, who hid in the shadows while following Jesus. But God had a plan. In death, Joseph of Arimathea gained the confidence to stop hiding. He went forward and presented himself. He took Jesus' body and buried it in his own tomb. A tomb reserved for himself as an affluent man in society. Jesus spent two days in that tomb before he rose triumphantly. Joseph's tomb was then returned to him.

Jesus' birthplace was a simple stable, but they buried Him among the wealthy in death to fulfill His purpose.

Do you feel anxious about life and the presence of evil? Hold tight to the Lord, for His purpose always prevails.

"Many are the plans in the mind of a man, but it is the purpose of the LORD that will stand" (Proverbs 19:21 ESV).

Just as I Am

Disabled Charlotte Elliott wrote the hymn *Just as I Am,* at her lowest. She wrote it when she thought she was most unworthy. Sure, I'm glad she did. The hymn has comforted many for centuries.

Just as I am, without one plea
But that Thy blood was shed for me
And that Thou bidst me come to Thee
Oh, Lamb of God, I come, I come

Just as I am, though tossed about
With many a conflict, many a doubt
Fighting and fears within without
Oh, Lamb of God, I come, I come
Ooh, just as I am, ooh, I come
Ooh, just as I am, oh Lamb of God, I come

Just as I am, Thou wilt receive
Wilt welcome, pardon, cleanse, relieve
Because Thy promise I believe
Oh, Lamb of God, I come, I come
Ooh, just as I am, ooh, I come
Ooh, just as I am, oh Lamb of God, I come
Oh lamb of God, I come

~Charlotte Elliott

The Lord God accepts us just as we are. So go to him today. He accepts returns. All you have to do is ask.

"For the LORD your God is God of gods and Lord of lords, the great God, mighty and awesome, who shows no partiality and accepts no bribes" (Deuteronomy 10:17 NIV).

What Happens When Your Goal and Dream Become Theirs?

In your own quiet corner, you lie at night. You dream about being in the Nationals. You work hard, and that dream finally becomes real. Then you contemplate the feasibility of the Olympics. Four years of hard work and sacrifices, and it comes through! Millions cheer with joy, and you cannot help but beam. Then, another four years to go higher Is it possible? Can you do it again? You get to work again but soon realize the dream is no longer yours. You feel like stepping back, but consider—what will they say? How will they react? But really, you no longer want that dream for yourself.

Is it worth it to deny yourself and go after 'their' goal? One can only think of the Olympics and the predicament of the athletes who compete. Usain Bolt was one. Armed with the birth name Bolt, he struck lightning as a little country boy. His natural gift blessed the world over several Olympic seasons, then he walked away to change careers. Many understood but were disappointed. They took vacations to support their country and have fun at blissful destinations. All while being entertained at the Olympics.

Your decision, your choice, let's emphasize. Whatever goal you choose, it is your choice and no one else's. Work hard for it. Make sacrifices, but in the end, if you are successful, it's yours. Naturally, the salary and benefits of all-expenses-paid trips are delicious, but soon you get tired and may not want 'it' anymore. That's when you need to stand firm. To get the negatives out of your head. To ditch the goal when it no longer motivates you. When it seems like a chore to get out of bed and you feel nauseated just thinking about it, know that's when it's time to move on.

But first, pray. But before you do, pray. Seek the Lord's guidance and direction. Ask Him to lead you on His path and next steps. Prepare yourself adequately. Making a significant change decision should not be taken lightly; it has consequences. So do it stealthily. Through prayer and following the Lord's leading, you will find satisfaction as you take the next step to follow His will.

"My goal is that they may be encouraged in heart and united in love, so that they may have the full riches of complete understanding, in order that they may know the mystery of God, namely, Christ" (Colossians 2:2 NIV).

PSALM 8

Lord, our Lord,
  how majestic is your name in all the earth!

You have set your glory
  in the heavens.
Through the praise of children and infants
  you have established a stronghold against
  your enemies,
  to silence the foe and the avenger.
When I consider your heavens,
  the work of your fingers,
the moon and the stars,
  which you have set in place,
what is mankind that you are mindful of them,
  human beings that you care for them?

You have made them a little lower than the
angels
  and crowned them with glory and honor.
You made them rulers over the works of your
hands;
  you put everything under their feet:
all flocks and herds,
  and the animals of the wild,
the birds in the sky,

and the fish in the sea,
all that swim the paths of the seas.

Lord, our Lord,
how majestic is your name in all the earth!

Igniting Hope: A Call to Courage and Resilience

God's Simple Asks

Have you played an online game where you must pay to continue playing after running out of turns? You can get additional time, but only after you invest resources such as time, money, or watch an advertisement.

At times, the Lord may ask us to do things (not for money) that seem too simple. We think He must be joking. We perceive that there must be a trick.

He instructed Naaman, the leper, to dip into the Jordan River seven times to cure his leprosy. He obeyed and was cured. We think of the Israelites, who were charged with marching around the city six times for six days. On the seventh day, they walked around the walls of Jericho and shouted. Guess what? The walls came down. Huh? Is that for real?

The widow of Zarephath, who was about to make the last meal to feed her child, was told to share her food with Elijah. By faith, without understanding, she shared her meal with the prophet. Her obedience resulted in an endless supply of food for them to eat.

To this day, we are still puzzled about how five loaves and two fish could have been enough to feed five thousand men, not to mention women and children. They even had bags of leftovers.

Spiritually, we are told to believe and ask the Lord to come into our lives. Some think this is way too simple, so they let it slide, ignoring the instructions for life eternal until it is too late. Some obeyed as they breathed their last breath, but the Lord welcomes all who diligently seek Him.

Today, have faith. Trust the Lord's instructions. The simplest things are what He uses to teach us to accept Him. Then, provide the instructions for our next steps toward spiritual growth.

"And without faith it is impossible to please God, because anyone who comes to him must believe that he exists and that he rewards those who earnestly seek him" (Hebrews 11:6 NIV).

Things Change

A compilation of research shared with me discussed the downfall of Kodak, whose name was once synonymous with photos but has now disappeared. Artificial intelligence has taken over the business.

We consider the likes of Uber, where a driver shows up at the click of a button to take you wherever you want to go. Vacation rentals offered by Airbnb have disrupted the hotel industry. Social media and devices recognize the faces of our friends, family, and colleagues without even a click or a whisper to search.

A politician missed the application deadline to run for office because she was busy networking to build her political base. Although she had a sizable number of willing supporters, she was disqualified after missing the application deadline. 'Tis sad.'

Things change, as the pandemic has clearly shown. We create goals and invest the time necessary for them to become real. But if we are not careful about monitoring our rapidly changing environment, we may discover that what we are working towards no longer exists.

Reflect and know that the Lord plants goals in our minds. Though the strategy to achieve it may change, we adapt through Christ. We confidently believe that every good and perfect gift comes from the Father of the heavenly lights, who is constant and unchanging. And because He does not change, we can stand by His assurance that He will remain the same and not change as technology does these days.

"Jesus Christ is the same yesterday and today and forever"
(Hebrews 13:8 NIV).

When Accidents of Purpose Redirect.

Get up and go. You can face any situation with him or without him. The choice is yours. ~Charles Stanley

I took some time to listen to my GreenLight audiobook while on a nature trek. Actually, it happened accidentally. I was listening to another audiobook about women of God, finished a few chapters, and moved on to another book. That's when I pounced upon my own GreenLight book and said, "Hmm, why not?" It has been a while since I've listened.

"Get up and go" was the tugging reminder of God's grace. Charles Stanley reminded us that we can face any situation with or without him. It's on track 4 if you already have the audiobook. If not, snatch yours. Paperback and Kindle are options, too.

The inspiration for the book came from God's word and His guidance. Follow His lead.

"I prayed to the LORD, and he answered me. He freed me from all my fears" (Psalm 34:4 NLT).

That Inner Feeling

The grave is filled with dreams that were never realized.
~Les Brown

Look closely at the inner feeling that quietly tugs at your heart. Listen quietly. You will hear. For years, my mom wanted to write her story. She wrote on notepads, pieces of paper, and the typewriter, then reached for the computer. A journey that lasted decades throughout her life, a journey that was never fulfilled.

My sister aspired to tell her story while suffering from cancer like a martyr. But like my mom, she too passed away with it in her heart, quietly waiting. She accomplished much, yet she still had that silent dream that was never fulfilled.

Years ago, I read the words of Habakkuk, which instructed, "Write what you see". Those words inspired me to write books, blogs, and articles on leadership, success, motivation, and inspiration. Listen carefully to the inner voice that tells you what to do with God's gift to you.

Through the guidance of the Holy Spirit, I write to inspire you to go after your dreams, goals, and aspirations.

"And we know that in all things God works for the good of those who love him, who have been called according to his purpose" (Romans 8:28 NIV).

In the Peace and Quiet of Solace

Solitude and peace create the perfect conditions for setting goals. I was reflecting on the different animals. Birds, insects, fish, and those that soar—our great, big, awesome God created all creatures. He did it in serenity, when the earth lacked form and was void.

And when it was done, he created man. The purpose? To enjoy His creations as told in Genesis. When making plans for today, tomorrow, or the future, do it with God. Only what's done for the Lord endures. Find that place of solace for your goal. Spend time with the Lord as you dream and create in silence. Then come out and reveal to others the great things He has done.

The things you do in silence will be unveiled at the right time. Let your light shine brightly.

"In the beginning God created the heavens and the earth. Then God said, "I give you every seed-bearing plant on the face of the whole earth and every tree that has fruit with seed in it. They will be yours for food. And to all the beasts of the earth and all the birds in the sky and all the creatures that move along the ground—everything that has the breath of life in it—I give every green plant for food." And it was so. God saw all that he had made, and it was very good. And there was evening, and there was morning— the sixth day" (Genesis 1:1, 29-31 NIV).

Ai and Virtuality

Hungry? Order a meal. It's not a problem; Uber delivers. Need a last-minute birthday gift? An outfit to go out on the town with a friend? These sure are no problem these days. Amazon delivers, and if you have Prime, that's even better. You get it the next day!

Smartphones, e-maps, and e-mail on the go— hitting the pause button during a movie—are things our little ones can't fathom living without.

Please don't call me. Text. WhatsApp? Despite having many channels on our big-screen TVs, we're still looking for the right one to watch. Netflix anyone?

Religious? Going to church? Overrated. That's a thing of the past. Thanks to the pandemic, there is a choice—meet online. Shut-ins are having a field day with church online, plus some of those who like convenience, but more on that another time.

These days, it seems that if you are tired, you can still drive. All you need to do is program your smart car to take you home—driverless, or so you think. I think you are on your own if the cops catch you. Not to mention artificial intelligence, which is becoming increasingly involved in our everyday lives. Just say what you want, and Siri and ChatGPT will run to your rescue. And we could go on and on.

What has our society come to? The Bible has been translated into so many versions that I can hardly recognize John 3:16 anymore. Some versions may have totally missed the meaning. But then again, who reads the Bible anymore? After all, we can listen to all those famous preachers on demand. Who needs to read when we can listen to what they want to share with us? Let the preachers read it and tell us.

Sigh, we have it all wrong. Our lives need the stillness and quietness that only come from reading the Word and listening to the still, small voice. Only then will we hear what the Bible says so that we can comfort those who are hurting and in pain. Only then will we be able to perceive what and how the good Lord wants us to lead others to Him for the peace He only provides. Only then will we be able to comfort those who mourn. Only then can we rejoice with those who shout with unspeakable joy when their blessings come through.

"Jesus Christ is the same yesterday and today and forever" *(Hebrews 13:8 NIV).*

Sunday Is Coming

Wait for it. Wait for it.

It was Friday. Sad day, or so we thought. Our performance of the crucifixion moved the congregation as we reenacted the soldiers' mocking nuances. Jesus, our Savior, died on the cross. Such humiliation should never be experienced. Tears flowed. He had died. Everyone felt hopeless.

Sunday

But then came Sunday! The discovery of an empty tomb provided a safe place for many. Delights, glee, joy, and praise rang out as the congregation worshiped aloud. The discovery of the empty tomb renewed hope.

Yes, Friday was sad. But together, we rejoiced as the promise shone brightly on Easter Sunday. He arose.

"Fret not yourself because of evildoers; be not envious of wrongdoers! For they will soon fade like the grass and wither like the green herb" (Psalm 37:1-2 NIV).

I See Walls

I see walls on every side of me.
Dark walls.
Brick walls.
Walls that are made out of steel and the
toughest stones.
I can't see my way through.
I'm overwhelmed

But then I am comforted knowing that you,
Lord, can see for me.
As I hold on to you,
You embrace me and hold me firm,
You comfort me with the words,
All will be well
Everything is going to be alright.

But still my heart longs for those days when I
don't have to worry.
Lord, you are in control and I long for your
quiet peace.
A peace that passes all understanding.
Unto you, I lift up my praise.
My heart yearns for you in a dry and thirsty
land.
For, with Christ in the vessel, I know I can
smile at the storm.

©Dr. Shelly Cameron

PSALM 87

He has founded his city on the holy mountain.
The Lord loves the gates of Zion
  more than all the other dwellings of Jacob.

Glorious things are said of you,
  city of God
I will record Rahab and Babylon
  among those who acknowledge me—
Philistia too, and Tyre, along with Cush—
  and will say, 'This one was born in Zion.'
Indeed, of Zion it will be said,
  "This one and that one were born in her,
  and the Most High himself will establish her."
The Lord will write in the register of the
peoples:
  "This one was born in Zion."

As they make music they will sing,

Fear: Confusion Is Nothing New

Fear of Dying with
Unaccomplished Dreams

"My greatest fear is dying without accomplishing my own dreams."

A middle-aged woman was deeply depressed. She had helped her children succeed in life. When they bought their first house, she was there. When they had their kids, she was there. A child needed to be picked up—she was there. However, through a series of events, she began reflecting. She got stuck and locked herself away from others. She loves her kids and is happy with their success, but her greatest fear is dying without accomplishing her dreams.

Aren't we like that at times? We are always there for others, to the detriment of our own dreams. We call those who step out and pursue their dreams without considering others selfish. The challenge is for us to find the right balance. The balance is remembering our goals, dreams, and aspirations while assisting those we care about in achieving their own.

God uses our dreams to communicate with us. He instills heartfelt goals and drives us to achieve them if we listen according to His will. We will only notice His directions if we listen or connect the dots. Often, our daily lives get so busy with stuff, be it family, friends, work, or being everything to everyone else, that we miss the essentials of His will.

Today, if you find yourself in that situation, attempt to pray. Seek the Lord's help. Ask him to lead you down the path He wants you to take.

"After these things the word of the LORD came to Abram in a vision: "Fear not, Abram, I am your shield; your reward shall be very great" (Genesis 15:1 ESV).

Have You Ever Been Afraid?

Ever been afraid? I have. I lived with my grandmother in a contemporary house when I was growing up. When I was ten years old, I passed the entrance exam to attend a prestigious high school. It was close to my parents' house, so I moved to live with them instead. The only problem was that the house was mid-century. Being close to school, I did not want the students to see where I lived because I feared they would tease me. So, for all of my high school years, I hid from them. Only close friends knew. I was popular in school because I participated in sports and other activities, which presented another challenge. That made things worse. I 'really' had to hide.

They condemned the house at the end of high school, which was a good thing. People love to stay in their comfort zones. My parents had no choice but to move.

Since then, there have been many other times when I have been afraid. Such as having my first child and making my first presentation to a big audience at work locally and then internationally. Not to mention when I jumped out of a plane doing a skydive!

But against that background, I have never let fear stop me from doing anything I want to do. I do things even when I'm afraid. Fear is my driver. I guess I owe that to that old house, or more so, to my relationship with God. It has encouraged me through the knowledge that all things work together for good and the confidence that when I am afraid, I will trust the Lord.

"When I am afraid, I put my trust in you" (Psalm 56:3 NIV).

Violence and CONFUSION Is Nothing New

Six shots all over the body, one shot to his head God said no. He died. She lived. Oh, what a tragedy. There are many stories like this about domestic abuse that leave us confused. Reports show that a majority of domestic violence cases go unreported. Murder suicides have also become common. As sad as it is, nothing surprises our great, big, awesome God. Sometimes He says no. Sometimes He says yes. But most important, Christ is all and in all. He is our refuge and strength.

Today, we pray for families going through issues of violence. We ask the Lord to comfort those who have become victims of violence and those who are mourning their loss. Yet, in all this, God remains in charge. He uses the bad things of this wretched world to achieve His purpose and plan for you.

Stay close. God cares for you.

"He will rescue them from oppression and violence, for precious is their blood in his sight" (Psalm 72:14 NIV).

When Fear Steps In

They said yes! You get the job of your dreams. You are thrilled. Life is good. Hmm, but what if it is a huge challenge? What if I can't do it? Then fear steps in.

You engage in a new entrepreneurial venture. You are excited. All seems well with your business idea. All plans fall perfectly into place. Then you wonder—can I, do it? What if I fail? Then fear steps in.

By chance, you meet the person of your dreams. You date. Get to know each other. Then comes the decision about marriage. A lifetime together. The prospect of a little 'mini-me' running around—oh, what joy! But then, what if that perfect dream person changes? The questions mull around in your head. Then fear steps in.

When fear takes over, what do you do? You face it head-on, that's what. Don't let it stop you. Do what you have to do. Take the plunge into your endeavor. Think positive. Gain knowledge. Build your confidence. There will always be good times and, yes, bad ones too. Enjoy the good. Don't fear the bad. It's called life. And life has its difficulties. It is your resilience that will help you get through—that will help you survive.

But most of all, pray. Take your fears, concerns, and cares to the Lord in prayer. He will work it out. He will quiet your spirit. Whatever you do, face your fear head-on with the faith that our Heavenly Father, the one and only true God, has provided.

"I will not fear though tens of thousands assail me on every side" (Psalm 3:6 NIV).

Plugged In?

I did some housework and rearranged things. After finishing, I reconnected the computer, laptop, and devices, but nothing worked. I figured that the electrical surge protector had gone wrong. So, I went to get another. When I plugged it in, I noticed that the other surge protector was just disconnected from the wall unit. I gasped, rolled my eyes, and connected it to the wall plug, and voila, it worked!

It caused me to reflect on our relationship with the Lord. We may lead groups, build relationships, and do many other things, but if we are not plugged into Christ as the source, then it makes no sense.

Take a moment today to evaluate your spiritual connection. Are you plugged in? Are you reading the Word and doing daily devotionals? Praying? All these contribute to our spiritual development. Without them, our actions are meaningless.

Stop and check the battery in your life. Don't miss the green light. Plug back in and experience the divine power from above.

"For the kingdom of God is not a matter of talk but of power" ~ (1 Corinthians 4:20 NIV).

And in the middle of my chaos, there you were.

~Unknown

Trapped

Trapped is how I feel

Trapped when the desires of my heart go unfulfilled.
Trapped when I rely on what the Lord has blessed others with.
Trapped, but grateful for God's provisions.

Trapped financially.
Trapped by mounting bills and rising fees.
Trapped by impatience.
Trapped by the ideas waiting to be born.
Trapped by age, status, and discrimination.
Trapped by life's restrictions.
Trapped within the confines of melancholic thinking.

Trapped, yet I know I can do all things through Christ.
Trapped by God's love, I still yearn for His swift rescue.
Trapped, yet embraced by God's grace and forgiveness.

PROVERBS 2:1-15

My son, if you accept my words
    and store up my commands within you,
turning your ear to wisdom
    and applying your heart to understanding—
indeed, if you call out for insight
    and cry aloud for understanding,
and if you look for it as for silver
    and search for it as for hidden treasure,
then you will understand the fear of the Lord
    and find the knowledge of God.
For the Lord gives wisdom;
    from his mouth come knowledge and
    understanding.
He holds success in store for the upright,
    he is a shield to those whose walk is
    blameless,
for he guards the course of the just
    and protects the way of his faithful ones.

Then you will understand what is right and
just
    and fair—every good path.
For wisdom will enter your heart,
    and knowledge will be pleasant to your soul.
Discretion will protect you,
    and understanding will guard you.

Wisdom will save you from the ways of wicked
men,
   from men whose words are perverse,
who have left the straight paths
   to walk in dark ways,
who delight in doing wrong
   and rejoice in the perverseness of evil,
whose paths are crooked
   and who are devious in their ways.

Have Faith, Hope and Trust

Sometimes It's a U-Turn

"If you haven't found it yet, keep looking."

This was a thought-provoking motivational quote shared on a social media platform. A curious patron followed up with the question, "But isn't it true that you should know when to go with the wave and when to let it go?" While responding briefly, I articulated in more depth.

Yes, you should indeed know when to go with the flow and when to let it go. In short, if it's a goal that you really want, there are many avenues to get there. Sometimes a U-turn is necessary. Sometimes it's a detour. Other times, it's a revamp. Same goal, different route. It makes sense, right? But delving deeper, let's examine each point.

Sometimes it's a U-turn.

Things happen. I remember writing what was supposed to be my first book, which actually turned out to be the fifth one published. My usual adage was to write about leadership, success, career, and personal development. However, this one was different. For the first time in my life, I couldn't figure out what type of book it was supposed to be. Then, one day, I made a U-turn. I went back to the beginning. I printed the manuscript, scattered it on the floor, and then sat and prayerfully examined what it was all about. That's when the Lord clarified that it was simply an inspirational book. It comprised short stories, exhortations, and encouraging prayers for challenging journeys.

The book GreenLight is available for purchase on Barnes and Noble, Amazon, and other places with positive reviews. Coincidentally, this book, titled RedLight, is the final in the series. The book GreenLight inspired a three-part series about the traffic light concept and how it applies to significant moments in our lives.

So, allow for the Holy Spirit's leading at different points in your life. Prayerfully sit. Be still. Listen and allow the Lord to direct your steps. Then, ask for His leadership and guidance as you step forward in obedience.

"Let the wise listen and add to their learning, and let the discerning get guidance" (Proverbs 1:5 NIV).

Sometimes a Detour

In pursuit of our goals, we encounter obstacles that force us off course. They force us to take a detour. Most often, we get angry, sad, or depressed. This happens most often when we're traveling. For me, it was my career. I started working in the financial industry. After six years, I lost my grandmother, the bedrock of my family. It took me on a whirlwind spin. I traveled to numb the pain.

After a year, I headed back to banking. At the time, it was seen as a 'prestigious job' and the only thing I knew. Soon after, I was steered to what I considered a small organization, which I thought was quite a bore. With no clear challenge, an opportunity arose within less than a week, and I returned to work in the bank. Days later, I was approached about an opportunity that existed. It turned out to be the same job. I rolled my eyes—not interested. A few weeks later, one of my close friends shared with me an opportunity outside of banking. I wasn't interested, but I humored her and went. Guess what? It was the same job!

Detour after detour routed me back to what I now know was the ideal job I was looking for, but because it was sealed in a different package,

I resisted. Also, what I perceived as a small organization was a subsidiary of the #2 international pharmaceutical company worldwide. I led their HR leadership portfolio in that region for over 14 years. Oh, what a detour!

Sometimes, you have to take a step back and connect the dots. Examine the pattern. What is the Lord saying to you? Where is He leading you? Seek His guidance with prayer to clarify His next steps for you.

"He guides the humble in what is right and teaches them his way" (Psalm 25:9 NIV).

Sometimes a Revamp

I love the movie *'Under the Tuscan Sun'*. In it, the main character, a well-known successful author, lost her life of success as she knew it. Her friend gave her a ticket to get away for a while. She eventually accepted—and on a whim, bought a house in Italy. A year later, it turned out to be a life change—a total revamp from what she was accustomed to. She became an entrepreneur, stepping out into the unknown, and it worked out for her. Same goal, but different space.

So yes, sometimes we have the same goal, but when things happen, it may force us to make a U-turn, detour, or a total revamp. Same goal, but a different route.

As Cally Logan encouraged:

God is a God of restoration and compassion, and He cares far more than we can even think or imagine about our lives individually. For so many, the unrest in our culture, and the unknowns of the future have left many feeling defeated, overwhelmed, or crushed in spirit.

Yet this is an instance in which we can turn our faces towards God, the God who splits seas, makes prisoners rulers, and defies death itself.

Together, we thank God for His forgiveness when we go astray, and more so, we praise Him for restoration. On bent knees, reach out to Him today. Tell Him all about your problem. He will set you free and steer you on the path to restoration.

"For this God is our God for ever and ever; he will be our guide even to the end" (Psalm 48:14 NIV).

Who Moved My...

I went to the grocery store that's been in the same locale for more than a decade. As I stepped in, the traditional fragrance of the familiar faces was missing. Confused, I inquired, "Where are they?" I was told that the owners sold the business and had moved to a different location for an improved venture. I felt cheated. Immediately, I decided I would go find them because—how could they do that to 'me'?

Then I started thinking about my passion. As a leadership coach, I daily encourage individuals to leap. To do what they have always wanted to do. Yet here I was, feeling cheated. How dare they?

Has that ever happened to you? We love the familiar. The thing that harmonizes and makes us comfortable and safe is tranquility. When it's gone, we feel a hollow in our lives—in our souls. I reflect on the book 'Who Moved My Cheese', which became famous for its simplicity yet profound impact. The late Spencer Johnson told the story of the change that takes place in a maze with amusing characters as they search for cheese. Its metaphorical delight draws us in as we identify with the characters. Those of us who sniff, scurry, and hem and haw at the sight of change.

Later, I returned to my usual self. It thrilled me that the management of that grocery store moved on. They left to achieve their dream. They had taken a bold step to higher heights.

Is there someone that you are blocking from achieving their goals? How about you? What is your own plan for the next 3–5 years? How will you get there? Step aside and allow yourself, your family, a friend, or a foe—yikes!—to achieve what you or they have always wanted.

But before you do, make sure you align your plans with God's will and purpose for your life. Don't plan without first prayerfully placing your thoughts and desires in the hands of God. Reflect on Peter, who, without asking the Lord, started defending Him in the Garden of Gethsemane. He cut off the soldier's ear and was rebuked by Jesus, who immediately healed him. Peter's plan was not God's plan.

So, take your goals, dreams, and desires to the Lord before acting on them. Ask for His intervention. He will lead you to the purpose and plans for your life according to His will.

"But their swords will pierce their own hearts, and their bows will be broken" (Psalm 37:15 NIV).

Stay in Faith, Don't Give Up

"Thank you, my dearest friend; you have made me a much better person than you know."

85-year-old reggae music matriarch Patricia Chin (Miss Pat) sent me this note. She planned a trip to Germany to promote her book, "The Reggae Music Journey," which she started writing in her early 80s.

Pastor Furtick's message about Abraham being 85 years old yet having the potential to achieve God's promise made me smile. Life is considered 'hard' by many at the age of 30, leading them to give up and fold their arms.

I will not lie. Sometimes, I'm tired physically, mentally, and spiritually. I find myself focusing on the problems that seem to envelop me, yet I can't solve them. But that's when I curl up in my weakness, pleading for the faith only the Lord provides.

But what is the difference between those who are living with purpose despite their age? Some say resilience. True, I agree, but more so, Christ. He makes us strong and gives us the strength to never give up. Today, stay in faith. Stay focused on prayer.

"For we walk by faith, not by sight" (2 Corinthians 5:7).

PSALM 42

As the deer pants for streams of water,
  so my soul pants for you, my God.
My soul thirsts for God, for the living God.
  When can I go and meet with God?
My tears have been my food
  day and night,
while people say to me all day long,
  "Where is your God?"
These things I remember
  as I pour out my soul:
how I used to go to the house of God
  under the protection of the Mighty One
with shouts of joy and praise
  among the festive throng.

Why, my soul, are you downcast?
  Why so disturbed within me?
Put your hope in God,
  for I will yet praise him,
  my Savior and my God.

My soul is downcast within me;
  therefore I will remember you
from the land of the Jordan,
  the heights of Hermon—from Mount Mizar.
Deep calls to deep

in the roar of your waterfalls;
all your waves and breakers
  have swept over me.

By day the Lord directs his love,
  at night his song is with me—
  a prayer to the God of my life.

I say to God my Rock, "Why have you forgotten
me?
Why must I go about mourning,
  oppressed by the enemy?"
My bones suffer mortal agony
  as my foes taunt me,
saying to me all day long, "Where is your God?"

Why, my soul, are you downcast?
  Why so disturbed within me?
Put your hope in God,
  for I will yet praise him,
  my Savior and my God.

Do All Things Through Christ

I Can Do All Things

I Can Do All Things through Christ

It's a mantra I teach my kids to pray whenever the going gets rough. It might be a test. Fear. A challenge or an endeavor. Whatever it is, God is always here. He is always nearby. So just whisper whenever you feel like giving up or becoming afraid.

I can do all things
I can do all things
I can do all things

I can do all things through Christ
I can do all things
Yes, I can do all things through Christ who gives me the strength

(Insert name) Can do all things through Christ

"I can do all this through him who gives me strength"
(Philippians 4:13 NIV).

The Fog

Fear gripped me. A 2-hour journey turned into three as clouds stormed. The foggy skies were comfortless. The visibility was almost null as the storm pounded. My headlights shone brightly as my hands held the steering wheel firm.

My commute slowed as my heart panicked. I prayed, then I prayed louder with a shout and asked, "What's happening, Lord?" Suddenly, the rain slowed. Though it didn't stop, I began to see the road ahead more clearly. Alone, I praised as I never had before. Highway praise!

Are you experiencing a season of storms in your life? Cling to our Heavenly Father. Pray without ceasing. When you cannot see what lies ahead, trust Him. He will work things out for your good.

"He guided them safely, so they were unafraid; but the sea engulfed their enemies" (Psalm 78:53 NIV).

The Very Thing That I Spent Years to Build Has Turned Out to Be My Worst Nightmare

'Tis sad'. As the middle-aged professional reflected, she realized that the very thing she sought, the thing she spent years building, the very thing that she depleted her resources for, turned out to be her worst nightmare. Education. Yes, it's education. She invested her resources in education. Every penny that she had, she invested in higher education. When that was done, she took out student loans. Her thinking? She would enjoy financial viability that would provide her with more than enough to cover her loans and allow her to live comfortably for the rest of her life.

Alarmed, she realized that it wasn't so—for the very thing she sought hid from her. They said she was too qualified! It made her weak to think of their mediocre thinking. People often reject the very qualities they seek in others, such as hard work, resilience, and dedication. Hmm, but is it what the Lord desires for my friend?

Jacob's wife Rachel begged God for a child, but it appeared God refused. For years, she prayed. Then she finally conceived and gave birth to Joseph, but died while giving birth to her second child, Benjamin. Was there a reason the spirit denied motherhood for so many years? Or was her purpose fulfilled through Joseph, who became an example of patience throughout the generations?

What about you? Is there something that the Lord has been denying you? Perhaps it's a relationship, delayed homeownership, or career—assets you have invested a lot of time and energy into, but now they've become your worst nightmare.

Despite the tough times that feel never-ending, there is a bright future ahead! Be encouraged never to give up. To fight the good fight. Things will get better. The revelation will come through prayer, resilience, and a continued fight for a better life. As you seek clarity in your path, you realize that things will get better one day.

Please don't do it alone. The Lord is nearby. Seek His guidance and leadership. He will lead you through the difficult times.

"Hope in the LORD and keep his way. He will exalt you to inherit the land; when the wicked are destroyed, you will see it" (Psalm 37:34 NIV).

Discouraged?

I often refer to the fictional Miss Havisham from the book Great Expectations. Left at the altar, she was determined to remain stuck for the rest of her life. She was afraid to move on. Decades later, she was still wearing her wedding dress.

Indeed, sad. But how many of us are like that? We lose a contract or a job, and we remain stuck, whining about the circumstances of the loss. We fall prey to a failed relationship and sit back for years—waiting, waiting, waiting. Someone did us wrong, and we complained about it for the rest of our lives. We fail to realize that we are only hurting ourselves since the person has moved on or sometimes does not even remember the circumstances.

If any of these situations pertain to you, shake it off. Move on. There's more in life for you if only you change your perspective.

There's a fictional cartoon of two men digging to find gold. Suddenly, one hits the jackpot! Hearing his screams of joy in the distance, the other turned away from his own, digging despondently. Onlookers were privy to seeing what was happening and realized that if only he had continued, he would have discovered that his own jackpot was right there. But sadly, he turned away and missed a tremendous opportunity.

How many of us are like that? When the going gets rough, you give up. Acquiring a degree or a certification is a challenging feat when the assignments pile up, when the work/life balance goes out of whack, when the child rebels, when the bills pile up, and when the panacea of sickness steps in when an ailing parent moves in. So many give up. Only to regret it later when things change.

So, how do you discern when to hold on? We hold on through God. He provides us with strength if we only pray and trust Him. He will love us despite our sins or our circumstances. We gain encouragement through praying, reading the word, and listening to His answers when they come. He leads and provides instructions on what to do, where to go, and what to say in all cases.

Allow yourself to be encouraged and keep holding on. Don't let go. Hold on until God tells you when to go. Be prepared for God to do exceedingly abundantly above all you could ask or think.

"LORD, the God of our fathers Abraham, Isaac and Israel, keep these desires and thoughts in the hearts of your people forever, and keep their hearts loyal to you" (1 Chronicles 29:18 NIV).

Write What You See

When God says go, obey, even when it makes little sense. As he did with Abraham, he often does not tell us how, when, or where. He just provides the green light and the nudge. If we are in tune, we will recognize his leadership.

Years ago, I felt his quiet guidance to write what I saw (Habakkuk). Since then, I have written encouraging words from the Lord to calm and guide the discouraged, the sick, and those needing reassurance. He has led aspiring authors who need my help to do the same. Indeed, I am humbled and will cling to Him.

Take His inspiration, and don't hesitate to step out, even when you're scared. Fear shouldn't stop you from doing what God has asked you to do. Don't trust your fear. It will hinder your progress.

Allow the Lord to be your safe place until He grants you the green light.

"Write, therefore, what you have seen, what is now and what will take place later" (Revelation 1:19 NIV).

PSALM 3

My son, do not forget my teaching,
　　but keep my commands in your heart,
for they will prolong your life many years
　　and bring you peace and prosperity.

Let love and faithfulness never leave you;
　　bind them around your neck,
　　write them on the tablet of your heart.
Then you will win favor and a good name
　　in the sight of God and man.

Trust in the Lord with all your heart
　　and lean not on your own understanding;
in all your ways submit to him,
　　and he will make your paths straight.

Do not be wise in your own eyes;
　　fear the Lord and shun evil.
This will bring health to your body
　　and nourishment to your bones.

Honor the Lord with your wealth,
　　with the firstfruits of all your crops;
then your barns will be filled to overflowing,
　　and your vats will brim over with new wine.

My son, do not despise the Lord's discipline,
    and do not resent his rebuke,
because the Lord disciplines those he loves,
    as a father the son he delights in.

Blessed are those who find wisdom,
    those who gain understanding,
for she is more profitable than silver
    and yields better returns than gold

Conquer as the Spirit Leads

Pre-planning Your Mistakes?

I heard a TV host who was showing a young lady how to use a piece of equipment, which she was actively trying to learn. She went into a series of what-if scenarios, to which he retorted with the question, "Are you pre-planning your mistakes?" She laughed.

It reminded me of how we often act. We think of everything that could go wrong instead of thinking of the things that could go right. What happens if I pursue entrepreneurship and fail? What if I apply for the job and they turn me down? What if I invest in the relationship and it doesn't work out? 'What-if' scenarios play over and over in our heads. It gets us nowhere. Get out of your head and take the bull by the horns (so to speak).

As the Lord did with so many biblical characters, He alone directs our path and instructs us where to go. Think of Jacob when the Lord instructed him to return home because of his fear and rift with his brother Esau, whom he fled from decades earlier. He obeyed, and a trusted relationship returned.

Will you just trust God?

"By day the Lord went ahead of them in a pillar of cloud to guide them on their way and by night in a pillar of fire to give them light, so that they could travel by day or night" (Exodus 13:21 NIV).

Giving Up

My eyes caught the attention of an article titled "Giving up." It quickly sparked my interest because I usually avoid ever giving up. In my youth, I did track, and for all those athletes out there, you know just how much effort it takes to get in shape. To stick to your goal. To become fit and ready for that race. As I advanced into maturity, the same held true for me. It became the very grain of my existence. During college and career advancement, I never gave up. As a coach, I motivate new entrepreneurs, managers, and employees to pursue their dreams and goals.

That article reminded me of another I had read about success and fear. Both fear and the desire to give up intertwine and cripple us, often fueling negative thoughts and actions. There are many individuals who throw away their lives, become lethargic, stuck, wasted, and stray away from their goals. They get into trouble and end up self-imprisoned, or worse.

Keep your spirits high. It is delightful to strive and reach for what you can achieve!

The writer of the article "Giving up" concluded with a twist. He suggested being wise enough to know when to stop, refuel, and get back on track.

I say, better yet, go back to the beginning. Seek the Lord's help and shake off that fear. Shake off the very thought of giving up. Ask God's guidance to apply the wisdom and strength needed to accomplish the desires He placed in your heart. After all, only what's done for the Lord will last.

"Take delight in the LORD, and he will give you the desires of your heart" (Psalm 37:4 NIV).

Suicide to Avoid the Pain?

Pain is a signal that something may be wrong. It is an unpleasant feeling, such as a prick, tingle, sting, burn, or ache. Pain may be sharp or dull. It may come and go, or it may be constant (National Library of Medicine).

Pain hurts. Pain causes discomfort and heartache; if it persists, it often drains those sick of the will to live. People do many things to avoid pain. Medications for relief can lead to addiction if used for a long time. Partying provides a misguided state of happiness while it lasts. People get lost in the music or drink to hide hurt, pain, boredom, or true feelings that might become clear to others. Not to mention taking drugs to numb emotions, tiredness, apathy, and more. These days, surgical procedures are common to get the perfect beach body to showcase socially or hide the inevitable progress of aging. Sexual thrills take some to a place of getting back at an unfaithful spouse or believing that another soul treasures them. All are temporary and lead to inevitable hurt and pain.

Suicide. This is the ultimate place of no return. What happens when it's done and they drift into another space of reality? Another place of accountability is a place of no return.

When the pain comes, and it will call out quietly or aloud—Jesus! He is our savior, protector, guide, and healer. The woman with the issue of blood quietly touched Jesus. Instantly, the Lord knew as she stepped forward in faith. She was healed. Years of suffering, pain, and embarrassment were gone in an instant. Through one touch.

In the same way, the disciples on the boat shouted, 'Lord save us!' Immediately, the wind, rain, storms, and clouds disappeared, leaving them puzzled. Peace returned to the seas.

Today, if your heart is in that place of unrest, that place where it seems no healing is in sight, guard against the superficial, temporary cures. Call out to the Lord quietly or aloud. Accept the peace that passes all understanding as He guards your heart in serenity and love.

"But as for me, afflicted and in pain— may your salvation, God, protect me" (Psalm 69:29 NIV).

Quiet Reflections

The ocean beat against the sandy shore with quiet movements. It is my safe place. I never want to leave. I sit coiled at the edge of the lazy beach chair, gazing in melancholy at the morning's sunrise. All is still as time stops. As the sun began its heated quest, I sat pensively, not wanting to leave.

Still fast asleep, there is no one in sight. Just me, as the waves batter the shore. My heart tugs as I long to get rid of life's woeful work-related stress. All I want is to stay and listen to nature's quest. In quietness is where Heaven awakens and gives me the strength to reach forward to start a new day, a new chapter, and a time of serenity. I pray I will listen as the spirit quietly leads, guides, and directs my path.

In stillness is where I find my strength. Strengthen me, Lord, strengthen me. Speak, and help me listen.

"He says, "Be still, and know that I am God; I will be exalted among the nations, I will be exalted in the earth" (Psalm 46:10 NIV).

Do Not Self-Reject...

Do not self-reject. Just don't do it.

Think about the last time an opportunity showed up. It may have been an entrepreneurial venture, a job, a relationship, or a personal move. It was too good to be true. So, you hesitated. Did your hesitation alter the result? Did you pursue it, or did fear paralyze you?

It's sad, but so often we self-reject. Often, we talk ourselves out of doing something we are well qualified for. Most common on the job front. We moved to a new area. Start the job hunt, and then when something big comes up, we feel we need to be more qualified. We look at the requirements and then decide we won't apply because we don't fit one or more of them. Or that company is too big; they would never hire me. We engage in typical self-talk, focus on the negative, and talk ourselves out of it.

What if questions arise? What if they see me in a different light? What if they think that I'm not good enough? What if they say no? Ditch the negative self-talk. What if they say yes? Send that email. Pursue what or who you consider essential to achieving your goal.

Life would be much easier if we focused on the positive. Ditch the self-pity. Ditch that negative self-talk. With God's help, go after your dream job, relationship, house, car, or vacation. Whoever God calls; He provides.

"Now may the God of peace, who through the blood of the eternal covenant brought back from the dead our Lord Jesus, that great Shepherd of the sheep, equip you with everything good for doing his will, and may he work in us what is pleasing to him, through Jesus Christ, to whom be glory for ever and ever. Amen" (Hebrews 13:20-21 NIV).

Ask the Lord's Guidance

Those were the words I saw on a list of things to do. My younger daughter wrote it. She was in graduate school, and, as most of us know, moving is a part of college life. While preparing to move, she had a checklist of tasks to complete, a habit instilled by her mother to ensure essential things were not overlooked when planning life's journey.

As I went to help clear an area in the kitchen, I pounced on a post-it with a list of things to do for the packing. On the list, I read the words "ask the Lord's guidance". Wow! As a mom, I was happy to see her give the Lord the place she needs in her life. My goal was to discreetly capture a picture of the list, but my phone was elsewhere. Later, I left and forgot to capture the treasure list.

We must seek the Lord's guidance in every aspect of our daily lives. We should not live without His directions, since only what is done for the Lord will last.

"Guide me in your truth and teach me, for you are God my Savior, and my hope is in you all day long" (Psalm 25:5 NIV).

Where Will It Lead?

Alex received a job offer for her dream job in another state, seven hours away from her family. As she advanced through the round of interviews, the prospective opportunity became more promising. They later invited Alex to do a final round of interviews with over two dozen senior managers. Excitedly, she flew to the state, did her interviews, and thought she nailed it. Nothing could go wrong—until it did.

Three days later, after flying back home and contemplating her next steps, she was told they went with the other candidate. She felt devastated. What did she do wrong? Simply—nothing. There was nothing she did wrong.

Life is a matter of choices, and every choice you make makes you ~John Maxwell.

Before making choices, we must consider where they will lead us. Is it marriage, first love, children, a new job, college, a new contract, or a new house? Always contemplate the future. Where will your choice lead you?

It's easy. Pray. Ponder wisely. Let faith guide you to make your decisions based on the spirit's direction. With God's help, Joseph succeeded in everything he did, even when he was falsely accused and imprisoned. We are advised to pray and let faith guide our decisions.

So, hold on to the Lord. Be confident in Him, and He will grant you success as you build your relationship with Him. May the Lord bless all your endeavors with success.

"If any of you lacks wisdom, you should ask God, who gives generously to all without finding fault, and it will be given to you" ~James 1:5 NIV.

Be Yourself But....

There is a craze going around with thoughts such as be you, be your best self, and you name it, it's yours. These are all centered on the "me craze." Everything is about being me, me, me. Live your best life! And yes, I understand the need to focus on ourselves.

But—and yes, there is always a but—there's a balance. Use caution. Be yourself, but be careful of your intake. This means that you should watch what you allow into your thoughts. It goes to your heart. When trying to please, undesirables can lead to negative emotions like apathy and sadness. Desirables create feelings of positivity, purity, and optimism. Make sure you follow the right crowd.

Yes, be you, but remain humble. Be Christ-centered, not self-centered. Be confident in who the Lord has made you to be. Ensure you walk circumspectly, as you are wise. It is a thin line, and you can fall off easily if you go astray.

"Have nothing to do with godless myths and old wives' tales; rather, train yourself to be godly" (1 Timothy 4:7 NIV).

Some Days

Some Days bring sunshine
Some days bring rain
Some days bring sorrow
Some days bring pain
Some days it's cold
Some days it's warm
Some days it's ferocious
Like a thunderstorm

Some days I cry and wallow in self-pity
Some days I sigh and say life is not pretty
Some days I get a jolt huge as a thunderbolt
Reminding me that I am blessed and praises to
God I should express

©Charmaine Allwood-Hanson

PSALM 61

Hear my cry, O God;
    listen to my prayer.

From the ends of the earth I call to you,
    I call as my heart grows faint;
    lead me to the rock that is higher than I.
For you have been my refuge,
    a strong tower against the foe.

I long to dwell in your tent forever
    and take refuge in the shelter of your wings.
For you, God, have heard my vows;
    you have given me the heritage of those who
    fear your name.

Increase the days of the king's life,
    his years for many generations.
May he be enthroned in God's presence forever;
    appoint your love and faithfulness to protect
    him.

Then I will ever sing in praise of your name
    and fulfill my vows day after day.

Solitude

The Thing About Being Alone

Contactless is a term that is described as not involving contact. Not requiring touching or interaction between people. The pandemic fueled opportunities for contactless commerce. The result—solo sadness, solo mourning, solo fears. Going solo means no one must know. But as often said, what's done in secret comes to light when those who are sad find themselves overwhelmed. The effects are the sad fruit of depression, which, when prolonged without treatment, can lead to feelings of wanting to give up. Sometimes, suicidal thoughts rear their ugly heads. And before we jump to say that couldn't happen to me, think about the signs of the rich and famous. Those who suffer in silence and feel that they cannot handle it anymore include travel enthusiast Anthony Bourdain, comedian Robin Williams, and Miss USA Cheslie Kryst, to name just a few. We join with their loved ones as they still mourn.

'Tis sad,' indeed. Our contactless society feeds on aloneness, even in a crowd. Let's do what we can together in our small corner to connect with those behind closed doors. And if they won't answer, that's when you counter with direct help. We can't ignore mental illness anymore and pretend it doesn't exist. Contact those trained to help.

Things we can do are:

- Shut up and listen.

- Pay attention. There is always a sign.

- Check in on friends who go quiet or are missing.

- Invade their privacy—but do it wisely, quietly, and cautiously.

- Be real. A genuine spirit can be felt just like the hypocritical ones (yikes).

- Don't be afraid to ask, "Are you okay?" It sounds simple, but it's the right thing to do.

- It works. Ask God for wisdom, guidance, and that spirit of discernment.

May this reflection motivate you to connect with a silent friend or loved one today. Allow them to see the Lord's comfort and healing through you.

"Shout for joy, you heavens; rejoice, you earth; burst into song, you mountains! For the LORD comforts his people and will have compassion on his afflicted ones" (Isaiah 49:13 NIV).

The Answer for Those Troubled

A pop-up alert busted through my work. One of my favorite dancers and entertainers, tWitch, was discovered dead in a hotel room. What? I blinked my eyes. Was I seeing right? tWitch? Who in Heaven's name could have harmed him? Second news alert. He did it himself! A single shot. You are lying! That is not true. How could they say that? He could not have. Shortly after, a note from his wife came with the words—they will dance. She will save the last dance for him.

A friend texted me hours later to inform me that an ex-coworker had unexpectedly passed away during a colonoscopy. I was still in disbelief. Very few succumb to that procedure, which is designed to check for problems before they arise. Subsequent chats came of a mom, a dad, and an uncle who the deadly disease cancer had snatched away. Separate circumstances, but just like my mom, sister, and grandmother, they had passed away. Their slow, difficult, and cancerous suffering had ended.

The deaths of our loved ones, friends, and family are inevitable. But sadly, daily reports of suicide ensue. Can we stop that mental disease? Are there signs? Is it possible to prevent it?

Jesus is the answer. Personally, sometimes the going gets rough. During those moments, I turn to the only one capable of relieving my hurts, pains, fears, and confusion about life's events. School shootings. Why take an innocent life? Why do children go astray? Families don't talk. Relatives fuss and feud. Not to mention couples who fight. Nowadays, divorce is common, and couples are encouraged to separate at the first sign of an issue to 'take care of themselves'. Trying to work things out is no longer encouraged. Go live across the street. Live nearby so children will not suffer 'too much'.

We scream and cry. Then ask, "What's wrong"? Then the still small voice of the Lord quiets our hearts, whispering, I am the answer. Jesus is the answer. Tell Him your woes, your misunderstandings, your weaknesses, and your fears.

Pray. Talk to Him. He will see you through. He will provide the strength needed during tough times. It may appear through a song, a friend, or a sign through a brief God wink. But we must be in tune. A supportive friend seeking help on your behalf, combined with prayer, can work wonders as our hearts hurt together. May strength and courage be yours through Christ.

Beyond judgment. Accept Christ. Accept help.

"Let each of you look not only to his own interests, but also to the interests of others" ~ Philippians 2:4 ESV.

The Influence of Dying for Likes

Yep, it's real. People are literally dying for likes. Social media has changed the world. A self-professed social media influencer lost her balance in an attempt at a baffling jump. She was unsuccessful, and the result was tragic. She died on impact.

Despite a category four hurricane warning for evacuation, a couple ventured into the sea and clung onto a gorge just to take a photo for the likes. And there are many more.

The ultimate sacrifice occurred when Christ died for the ungodly. He willingly gave His life for you and me while we were yet sinners. We did not deserve His sacrificial death on the cross, but He did it anyway.

Let us be like Christ and live our lives not for the likes but for the love.

"And when you pray, do not be like the hypocrites, for they love to pray standing in the synagogues and on the street corners to be seen by others. Truly I tell you, they have received their reward in full" ~ Matthew 6:5 NIV.

Waiting Is What I Do...

I'll wait for You as long as You want me to. I'll wait until it's your time.
I'll wait until You say yes.
I'll wait because I want nothing less than your will.
I'll wait on your direction,
I'll wait on your leading,
I'll wait on your guidance.

And when I get impatient, Lord, hold my hand and make me stronger than I am. z
Yes, I'll wait Lord, I'll wait.

"Wait for the LORD; be strong and take heart and wait for the LORD" ~ Psalm 27:14 NIV.

Alone at Last

A frustrated woman shared how tired she was. I inquired about the last time she was alone. She could not recall. It had been years (if ever). Two weeks later, she shared that she had found a cabin in the woods to which she couldn't wait to get away. The thought calmed her while she experienced the anticipation of being alone at last.

Jesus did that. Many times, during His time on earth, He asked His disciples to come away to a quiet place to pray. To restore our communion with our Heavenly Father.

How about you? When was the last time you had some quiet time to yourself? To reconnect with our Heavenly Father and listen to your own thoughts and dreams?

"So they went away by themselves in a boat to a solitary place" ~ *Mark 6:32 NIV.*

PSALMS 62

Truly my soul finds rest in God;
  my salvation comes from him.
Truly he is my rock and my salvation;
  he is my fortress, I will never be shaken.

How long will you assault me?
  Would all of you throw me down—
  this leaning wall, this tottering fence?
Surely they intend to topple me
  from my lofty place;
  they take delight in lies.
With their mouths they bless,
  but in their hearts they curse.

Yes, my soul, find rest in God;
  my hope comes from him.
Truly he is my rock and my salvation;
  he is my fortress, I will not be shaken.
My salvation and my honor depend on God
  he is my mighty rock, my refuge.
Trust in him at all times, you people;
  pour out your hearts to him,
  for God is our refuge.

Surely the lowborn are but a breath,
  the highborn are but a lie.

If weighed on a balance, they are nothing;
  together they are only a breath.
Do not trust in extortion
  or put vain hope in stolen goods;
though your riches increase,
  do not set your heart on them.

One thing God has spoken,
  two things I have heard:
"Power belongs to you, God,
and with you, Lord, is unfailing love";
and, "You reward everyone
  according to what they have done."

The Power of Prayer

A Little Prayer for You...

May the Lord wrap His loving arms around you.

May He take away your pain and discomfort.

May He provide joy deep within.

May He grant you more good days than bad.

May He grant you quiet solace.

May He always bless and keep you.

May He always bless you in overflow.

"May your eyes be open toward this temple day and night, this place of which you said you would put your Name there. May you hear the prayer your servant prays toward this place" ~ *2 Chronicles 6:20 NIV.*

He Is Here

Every time we went to church, the congregation sang the senior pastor's preferred chorus. Boy, were we tired of hearing it every time we went to church? Then, one day, I took the time to listen to the lyrics:

> He is here, Hallelujah!
> He is here, Amen!
> He is here, Holy, Holy
> I will bless His name again
> He is here, listen closely
> Hear Him calling out your name
> He is here, you can touch Him
> You will never be the same

Just think of it. God is present with us no matter where we go. Jonah was in the belly of a fish. Hagar, who mocked Sarah and whom Abraham banished to the wilderness, Hagar cried out, and there He was. Our great God came to her rescue. And we can think of many examples, such as the three Hebrew boys—Shadrach, Meshach, and Abednego—who defied the king's order to worship the golden idol and were thrown into the fire. Yet God saved them, and it did not consume them.

God is always here. He is near. So, if you are going through difficulties, call out to Him right now. Don't try to do it alone. Ask for His help. He will be happy to comfort, lead, and guide you.

"The LORD is near to all who call on him, to all who call on him in truth" ~ *Psalm 145:18 NIV.*

A Prayer for the Sick and Hurting...

In all things we give thanks

When we don't know what to do, Father, you do.
When we don't know what to Say, speak through us.
If silence is all we have, help us not to fear it, but receive it.
Grant us comfort and strengthen our hearts while we wait.

When we are far away from our ailing loved ones, you're there. You're nearby.
When we feel helpless, grant wisdom.
When we are perplexed, grant clarity

Father, please intervene as only you can.
Please quiet all hearts right now.
Grant comfort, quiet peace to the entire family's anxious soul.
Intervene now, Lord, as only you can.
Please intervene.

Take care of the Ailing's body and spirit
Take care of the family.
Take care of the caregiver's anxious mind.

We pray for these things in your name.
Intervene Lord, intervene.
Intervene as only you can.

"See, I am doing a new thing! Now it springs up; do you not perceive it?" ~ Isaiah 43:19 NIV.

A Prayer of CONGRATULATIONS

You made it because you have what it takes to win. It is my prayer that the Lord will continue to:

Convert your discomfort to comfort
Your pains to gains
Your minimum to maximum
Your losses to profits
Your Tears to smiles
Your sorrow to pleasures
Your bad-wiser to well-wiser
Your debts to credits
Good dreams to realities
And make these everlasting
I'll always Love you
I am Proud of you

© Elaine Cameron-Walters (deceased)

Rescue Me...

Rescue me, Lord, rescue me. Often, it seems You take so long to come to our rescue, but your timing is always right. So, we will wait for You just as long as You want us to. We only ask this one question, Lord, that You strengthen us while we wait expectantly because we cannot do it alone.

But we know You are our safe place, and in You we trust all day long.

May we find solace in the assurance that God knows when to send us what we need.

"Even to your old age and gray hairs, I am he, I am he who will sustain you. I have made you and I will carry you; I will sustain you and I will rescue you" ~ Isaiah 46:4 NIV.

Manna in the Desert

It's funny how the Lord poured down manna in the middle of the desert. The desert is a dry place where nothing lives. Yet it's unfathomable how He provided food for an entire nation for 40 years.

And He did it when he promised, on time. Those who gathered too little had enough, and those who gathered much did not have too much.

Today, may you and I trust God, always in every circumstance. Remember, He will provide more than we could ever ask or think because nothing is too hard for the Lord, and we know we can do all things through Christ. He will provide the strength and courage needed.

"Don't worry about anything; instead, pray about everything. Tell God what you need, and thank him for all he has done. Then you will experience God's peace, which exceeds anything we can understand. His peace will guard your hearts and minds as you live in Christ Jesus" ~Philippians 4:6-7 NLT.

"He said to them, "Come with me by yourselves to a quiet place and get some rest"

~ Mark 6:31 NIV.

Your Body Is the Temple.
Treat It Right....

Your body is His temple.
Treat it right. Exercise. Eat right.
Think pure thoughts.
Breathe.
Inhale positivity.
Exhale negativity.
Read the Word.
Let it sink in.

"Do you not know that your bodies are temples of the Holy Spirit, who is in you, whom you have received from God? You are not your own" ~ *1 Corinthians 6:19.*

Inexplicable Faith: Embracing Hope and Trust in Christ

Amid towering bills that threaten to cast shadows over our lives, persistent sickness that challenges our spirits, and the heartache of watching loved ones stray from their path, hope emerges as a beacon. Its hope is anchored in Christ's promise, which whispers through the valleys of uncertainty: "Fear not, for I am with you."

When relationships stand stagnant, and the weight of depression lingers heavily, there's a refuge—a sanctuary where we find solace. We find that sanctuary in God, the One who is our strength in moments of weakness. A profound truth emerges through the trials: Tomorrow will find its care in Christ's embrace.

On this journey, bent knees meet hallowed ground. Prayer becomes our refuge. With unwavering faith, we turn to God, our provider, known as Jehovah Jireh. Each plea is a testament to our reliance on Christ and a recognition that all we have is Him. In the symphony of our lives, we pray for Jesus to intervene, to be the compass guiding us through the storms.

You, Lord, are our safe harbor—a refuge where fear dissolves and where hope finds its haven. Faced with life's inexplicable moments, we find solace in Christ's embrace. In times of despair, the power of Christ's presence is our cornerstone.

"Even to your old age and gray hairs I am he, I am he who will sustain you" ~Isaiah 46:4 NIV.

Prayer Checklist

I think of Sergio's family, who lived in the building that came crashing down in Miami. A building labeled as a catastrophe (unknown to residents). It claimed the lives of over one hundred people while they slept. Immediately, people of faith prayed and prayed. They pleaded with God for the safe survival of those affected. Sadly, it was too much, and after 14 days, searchers resorted to a rescue mission instead to retrieve the remains of the fatalities. This was a national crisis acknowledged by community leaders up to the President of the United States. Such catastrophes may not be easily forgotten as we remain on our knees.

I also think about Hailey's mother, who had a degenerative illness. Similarly, Ken's brother was admitted to the hospital for prolonged treatment, while Laila felt discouraged as she could not find a job.

Common to these scenarios is that they all asked friends, colleagues, and the church to pray. Many joined in prayer at the onset but, as time passed, forgot to pray and only remembered intermittently. Life's daily priorities often overshadow even the most devastating catastrophes as they linger.

That's where a prayer checklist comes in. It serves as a basis for times when there's too much to remember. We forget to pray for the sick, struggling relationships, the unemployed, the discouraged, and our own needs, even with good intentions. Let's not forget how often we forget to give thanks for answered prayers.

A prayer list is invaluable. Here are a few reasons:

1. It helps us remember what and for whom to pray.

2. When God answers prayers, it gives us a reason to offer praise and thanksgiving.

3. It provides a medium for reflection when we reflect on what the Lord has done.

4. It is a way to acknowledge our journey with God. Often, He had to carry us. At other times, He provided comfort. Sometimes, we reflect and cannot comprehend how we made it through. During our challenging times, He strengthened us.

5. When we reflect, a prayer list serves as a year-end dialogue with family and friends.

Start capturing your prayer requests today. An e-notepad (smartphone) or a simple sheet of paper will do, but a prayer journal will help to keep them more organized. You can get them at most pharmacies, grocery stores, and convenience stores. GreenLight, which is the first book in this series, also has a prayer journal, which will help.

Reflect on the many needs that have crossed your path. Would a prayer checklist help? Something to think about as we approach the Lord in daily prayer.

"Hear my prayer, LORD, listen to my cry for help; do not be deaf to my weeping" ~ Psalm 39:12 NIV.

You never waste time waiting on God.

~ Charles Stanley

PSALM 23

The Lord is my shepherd, I lack nothing.
He makes me lie down in green pastures,
he leads me beside quiet waters,
he refreshes my soul.
He guides me along the right paths
   for his name's sake.
Even though I walk
   through the darkest valley,
I will fear no evil,
   for you are with me;
your rod and your staff,
   they comfort me.

You prepare a table before me
   in the presence of my enemies.
You anoint my head with oil;
   my cup overflows.
Surely your goodness and love will follow me
   all the days of my life,
and I will dwell in the house of the Lord
   forever.

Give Thanks

New Beginnings. New Hope.

Most individuals feel hopeful when a new beginning is on the horizon. Our deepest desire is never to go through that wretched pandemic year again. To me, the most important things in life are giving thanks and keeping hope alive. Having said that:

I wish you health.

I wish you satisfied needs beyond what is required.

I wish you abundance to share with others.

I wish you long-lasting smiles that reach deep inside.

I wish you years filled with extravagant laughter.

But most of all, I wish you peace that only the spirit can provide.

I hope you find solace in holding onto the only one with firm support.

"Oh, that I might have my request, that God would grant what I hope for" ~Job 6:8 NIV.

Quiet Nudges in the Chaos

In the relentless whirlwind of life's demands, a sacred sanctuary beckons to us. It is a place where the soul finds solace amidst the chaos, a respite for the heart in a world that never ceases its clamor. It is a place we often overlook, overshadowed by the noise of our daily routines. But within this overlooked refuge lies a power that can transform our existence.

As we journey through the bustling tapestry of life, the demands of work, family, and ambition threaten to pull us further from our spiritual core. Yet, despite the loud distractions, the Lord's presence persists as a beacon of hope and guidance.

Amidst the whirlwind, we discover the art of making time—precious moments carved out from the cluttered hours of our lives. Here, in the silent embrace of solitude, we find His company. In those still, small moments, we uncover a calmness only the Divine can offer—a balm for our restless souls.

As we venture deeper into this spiritual odyssey, we uncover the power of prayer, the thread that weaves our lives into the divine tapestry of creation. It is a lifeline to the Heavens, a lifeline that, amidst the hustle and bustle, we may momentarily forget. Yet the Lord is patient; His grace is boundless, gently nudging us back to our place of communion.

My heart is filled with gratitude, Lord, for your unwavering patience and grace, even when I falter. In these words, we find the essence of our journey. It is a journey of gratitude, of humble acknowledgment of our own imperfections, and of the unending love of our Creator.

"But the eyes of the LORD are on those who fear him, on those whose hope is in his unfailing love" ~Psalm 33:18 NIV.

One Person Can Make a Difference

Dr. Vivienne Kerr's unexpected passing deeply saddened me, despite never meeting her in person. She was so alive. The doctoral student who found me on NSU's university page aspired to write her own book. She played an essential role in my life without her knowledge. The book she wrote affected many people.

We developed a professional relationship over time as she strode through life's changes. Although it broke my heart, she passed away peacefully in her sleep. It reminds us to make a difference in life and to always be prepared since we never know when our time will come.

"No good thing does he withhold from those who walk uprightly" ~Psalm 84:11 ESV.

The Blessing

The Lord bless you and keep you
Make His face shine upon you and be gracious
to you
The Lord turn His face toward you
And give you peace

May His favor be upon you
And a thousand generations
And your family and your children
And their children, and their children

May His presence go before you
And behind you, and beside you
All around you, and within you
He is with you, he is with you
In the morning, in the evening
In your coming, and your going
In your weeping, and rejoicing

He is for you, he is for you
Amen, amen, amen

© Musixmatch

PSALM 100

Shout for joy to the Lord, all the earth.
Worship the Lord with gladness;
come before him with joyful songs.
Know that the Lord is God.
It is he who made us, and we are his
we are his people, the sheep of his pasture.

Enter his gates with thanksgiving
and his courts with praise;
give thanks to him and praise his name.
For the Lord is good and his love endures
forever;
   his faithfulness continues through all
   generations

Reset

6 Tips for a Spiritual Solo Retreat

To retreat means to withdraw. To take a step back. Jesus did this many times. He would disappear to spend time in the presence of His Father. He wanted to quiet His heart to gain the strength needed for the next steps on His earthly journey. If He needed strength, how much more do we? Shouldn't we follow the example that He set?

Larissa Marks, a HuffPost contributor, provided six practical steps for making a spiritual retreat. Here, I share while giving a few of my comments.

1. **Create the time and find a place.** Any quiet place will do. It may be in your home or someplace far away. It may be at a monastery or in nature. For me, I skipped home to get away from the distractions. I finally gave in after two decades of receiving a nudge to go. Just me. Solo.

2. **Set your intentions**. What is the purpose? What is it you would like to achieve from this time with Him? Is it a call? Is it a life decision that you need to make? For me, it was discernment and following His lead for the next phase of my life.

3. **Settle into God's presence**. Do something that quiets your heart and eases you into His presence. For me, it's walking in nature or sitting quietly, breathing, welcoming, and experiencing His presence. Ask Him what He wants you to receive. Listen and follow His lead.

4. **Reflect**. Do some quiet reflection. What's been your experience in recent weeks, months, or years? What's been exhausting you? What has satisfied you?

5. **Connect with God**. Read scripture. Notice any desire(s) that emerges. For me, there's always a fullness of joy in His presence. Even amid life's storms, I can experience His quiet peace.

6. **Receive and return**. Think about what you received during this time away. What do you want to stop doing or start doing? Remember, it's not about you; it's about the Lord and accomplishing His will and purpose for your life.

I hope these tips will help provide guidance as you make important life decisions or seek discernment for the next phase of your life. If you have done solo retreats, what did you walk away with? What stood out most about this experience? Reflect and share with a friend who can benefit.

"He maketh me to lie down in green pastures: He leadeth me beside the still waters. He restores my soul" ~Psalm 23:2 KJV.

Nature's Getaway

By the sea, I couldn't wait to sit casually on the sand. Me, my towel, my book, and the birds were all in one as the mighty waves thundered and splashed against the seashore. The weather forecast said it would be the coldest day of the season. Disappointment soared at the spoiled prospect, yet I was still determined to chill (literally).

I sat still, gazing into the distance. Cold yet relaxed. It was as if there was not a care in the world. I watched the little bird hunt its food, fighting against the rushing waves as they eroded the shore. "Give up!" I shouted. But it did not, as it tried repeatedly to grab another peck and another peck. Its little body was no match for the cold, windy weather, but it was yet to give up. Nature at its finest.

Have you ever noticed that when we crave a break, short or long, we seek solace in nature? Sometimes, we seek refuge in water activities like boating, kayaking, and scuba diving that are available at the beach. At other times, we retreat to the woods while camping. Solitude retreats and long meadow walks are also things we choose to do.

Whatever our choice, let us ponder in silence as we reflect on nature's quiet existence. Let us use our time away to reconnect with God and gain the periodic reset we need to boost our next steps.

Today, take time to look around you. The birds and bees speak of the Lord's glorious creation. Oh, come, let us adore Him!

"Forget the former things; do not dwell on the past. See I am doing a new thing. Now it springs up; do you not perceive it? I am making a way in the wilderness and streams in the wasteland" ~Isaiah 43:18-19

He Is My Peace

The cleft is my favorite place to be. This temporary space helps me hide from my infirmities, wants, needs, and desires.

Beneath the shadows, I lie in wait for the Lord's amazing answers. In between, He comforts, leads, and guides. He grants me peace and quiet solace as I wait (though often impatiently). Pace, growth, love, and understanding are all He asks.

He is my peace. I hope He's yours too.

"He heals the brokenhearted and binds up their wounds"
~Psalms 147:3 NIV.

Peace in the Midst

May we experience Peace:

Peace in the midst of chaos
Peace in the midst of struggle
Peace when things get out of hand
Peace during mayhem
Peace during lack
Peace in courage
Peace in times of Fear
Peace in times of confusion
Peace in sickness
Peace in health
Peace in quiet time
Peace in ease

May we always experience peace. A peace that only our Lord can provide. He is my peace. Hope he's yours too.

Hiding

At noon we hide under the cover
We hide as the problems hover
We hide in Christ's Safe Place
We hide in His beloved Space
We hide until the problems are gone
We hide until things get back to Norm
At noon we hide
We hide until the problems sever

PROVERBS 1:1-7

The proverbs of Solomon son of David, king of
Israel:
for gaining wisdom and instruction;
   for understanding words of insight;
for receiving instruction in prudent behavior,
   doing what is right and just and fair;
for giving prudence to those who are simple,
   knowledge and discretion to the young—
let the wise listen and add to their learning,
   and let the discerning get guidance—
for understanding proverbs and parables,
   the sayings and riddles of the wise.

The fear of the Lord is the beginning of
knowledge,
   but fools despise wisdom and instruction.

"It is finished"

~ John 19:30 NIV

Resources

Teachers of the Truth

Many false teachings exist today. Here is a list of those who preach the truth of the bible collated by Pastor Mike Wiggins, Calvary Chapel, PSL.

Adrian Rogers
John MacArthur
Charles Ryrie
John Phillips
Charles Stanley
John Walvoord
Chuck Swindoll
Norman Geisler
Chuck Smith
Robert Lightner
David Guzik
Skip Heitzig
David Jeremiah
Dr. Tommy lce
Dwight Pentecost
Tony Evans
Ed Hindson
Warren Wiersbe
Greg Laurie

GotQuestions.org

Prayer For Salvation

God, I admit that I can't continue going through life without you. I need you, and I want you to change me. Please forgive me for all the mistakes I have made. Take away the guilt and shame I have been carrying and make me brand new.

I believe that Jesus died for me and rose again so that I could live for you and with you. So please fill me with your Holy Spirit and make me eager to serve and follow you for the rest of my life.

Today my life is no longer my own—I give it to you. I accept your free gift of salvation and I welcome you into my everyday life.

Thank you for transforming me!

In Jesus' name, Amen.

15 Verses to Fight Fear

1. All of you be quiet before the Lord. For He is coming from His holy place (Zachariah 2:13)

2. Write it down because I want the faithful to be encouraged (Habakkuk 2:2)

3. Wait on the Lord: be of good courage, and he shall strengthen thine heart: wait, I say, on the Lord (Psalm 27:14)

4. No good thing does He withhold from those who walk uprightly (Psalm 84:11).

5. Don't fear, for I have redeemed you; I have called you by name; you are Mine. (Isaiah 43:1)

6. So do not fear, for I am with you; do not be dismayed, for I am your God. I will strengthen you and help you; I will uphold you with my righteous right hand. (Isaiah 41:10)

7. For God has not given us a spirit of fear, but of power and of love and of a sound mind. (2 Timothy 1:7)

8. Have I not commanded you? Be strong and courageous. Do not be terrified; do not be discouraged, for the Lord your God will be with you wherever you go. (Joshua 1:9)

9. Therefore, do not worry about tomorrow, for tomorrow will worry about itself. Each day has enough trouble of its own. (Matthew 6:34)

10. Even though I walk through the darkest valley, I will fear no evil, for you are with me; your rod and your staff, they comfort me (Psalm 23:4)

11. Who, then, are those who fear the Lord? He will instruct them in the ways they should choose (Psalm 25:12)

12. The Lord confides in those who fear him; he makes his covenant known to them (Psalm 25:14)

13. Though an army besiege me, my heart will not fear; though war break out against me, even then I will be confident (Psalm 27:3)

14. The angel of the Lord encamps around those who fear him, and he delivers them (Psalm 34:7)

15. Therefore we will not fear, though the earth give way and the mountains fall into the heart of the sea (Psalm 46:2).

Other Books
by Dr Shelly Cameron

The Leadership Challenge: Caribbean
American Leaders in the United States
Published in the Journal of American Academy
of Business Cambridge (JAABC)

Success Strategies of Caribbean American
Leaders in the United States
Success Strategies of Immigrant Leaders in the
United States

A Review of Women Immigrants and The
Challenges Face: Perspectives on Higher
Education in the United States *Co-Authored
with Dr Indiana Robinson*

Your Career. Ditch It. Switch It
Success Strategies Workbook

GreenLight: When God Says Go
My Safe Place Is With You Lord
RedLight: When God Says No
GreenLight Journal
RedLight Journal

101+ Empowering Quotes For New
Entrepreneurs
Motivational Quotes To Boost Your Success

About the Author

Dr. Shelly Cameron is the Founder of the Global Coaching Corner. She has over two decades of experience in coaching C-Suite executives and multi-generational professionals. Dr. Shelly honed her people management skills while working for a big pharmaceutical company for over a decade. She worked in the CARICAM region and collaborated with Latin American countries. These days her work includes coaching developing leaders in Canada, the USA, countries throughout the Caribbean / CARICOM region.

Dr. Cameron has a strong record of accomplishment in diverse industries. She has a Doctorate in Organizational Leadership and Masters in Health Administration and HR Management. Dr. Shelly is a published author and accredited Master Coach. Her study with Nova Southeastern University focused on leadership strategies used by successful leaders. The study was published in JAABC Business Journal.

She has written books on leadership, career development, success, motivation, and inspiration. She's a member of the South Florida Authors of Color and the Florida Writers Association.

Dr. Shelly served 4 terms as Vice President and Board Member of HHRABC in Florida and is on the Program board of The Institute of Caribbean Studies in Washington DC. She is a member of the International Coaching Federation (ICF), ICF South Florida Chapter.

Dr. Cameron has a passion for people development and writes to inspire personal, professional, and spiritual growth. She strongly believes in prayer and has gone as far as Kenya, East Africa, to share its importance to personal and spiritual growth. She holds firmly to the stance that all things are possible with God.

When not writing, Shelly enjoys wave-watching, movies, reading and spending time with family.

10-Year-Old RJ's Written Napkin Note to Write this book

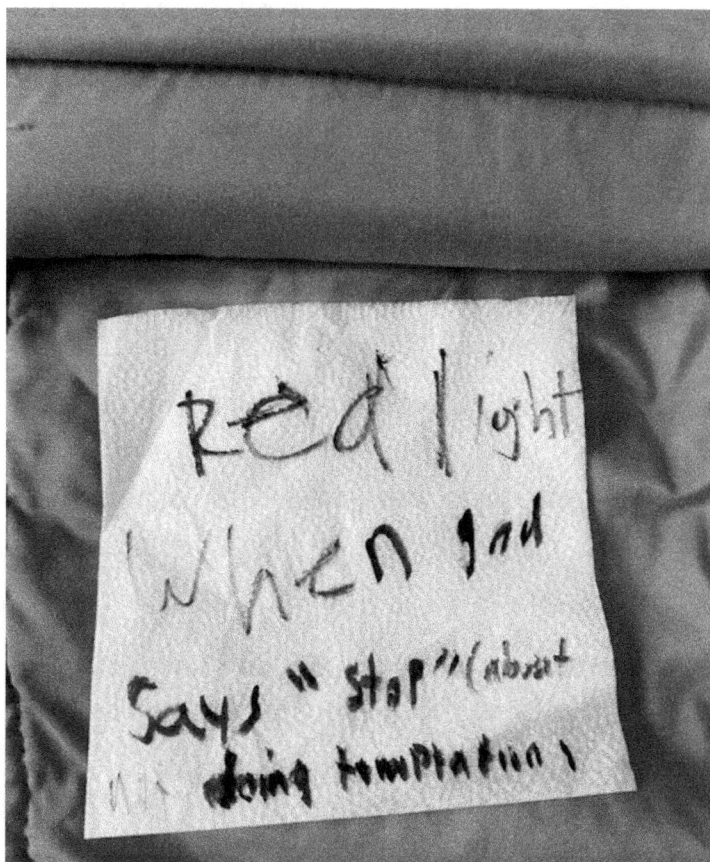

Thanks for Reading!

GreenLight Series exists to encourage the downhearted with the Comforts of the Holy Spirit's prodding.

If you appreciated this book, please let others know

- Pick up another copy to give as a gift.

- Share a link to the book or mention it on social media.

- Write a review on your blog, on a bookseller's website or on my site (ccahr.com, shellycameron.com, successfulleaders.net).

- Recommend this book to your church, book club or small group.

Connect and follow me on Instagram, Facebook, YouTube or LinkedIn

www.shellycameron.com/books | www.ccahr.com